JAZZ STANDARDS
FOR
DRUMSET

A COMPREHENSIVE GUIDE TO AUTHENTIC JAZZ PLAYING
USING 12 MUST-KNOW TUNES

BY BRIAN FULLEN

ISBN 978-0-634-06551-4

HAL•LEONARD®
7777 W. BLUEMOUND RD. P.O. BOX 13819 MILWAUKEE, WI 53213

In Australia contact:
Hal Leonard Australia Pty. Ltd.
4 Lentara Court
Cheltenham, Victoria, 3192 Australia
Email: ausadmin@halleonard.com.au

Visit Hal Leonard Online at
www.halleonard.com

ABOUT THE AUTHOR

Brian Fullen has been a veteran drummer in the Nashville music scene for several years, including world tours with SheDaisy, Shania Twain, Bob Carlisle, Peter Frampton, Allies, and the Imperials. He has also performed extensively with the artists Vince Gill, Michael Bolton, Wayne Brady, B.J. Thomas, Sierra, Jessica Andrews, Larry Carlton, Andy Griggs, Pete Huttlinger, and Identical Strangers, among others. In addition, he can be heard on the *Jack Frost* movie soundtrack, as well as commercials for the FOX Network, Chevrolet, Harley Davidson, and UPN.

As an educator, Brian has authored two critically acclaimed books, *Bass Drum Essentials for the Drumset* (Alfred Pub., co-authored with Dave Black), and *Contemporary Country Styles for the Drummer and Bassist* (Alfred Pub.). He is also a contributing author to *Modern Drummer* and *Percussive Notes* magazines, and teaches part-time at Belmont University in Nashville. Brian has given clinics and master classes for some of the most prestigious drum and percussion workshops and music schools in the country, including PASIC 1996 and 2001, PAS Day of Percussion Events, Berklee College of Music, and the University of North Texas College of Music.

Brian Fullen proudly endorses the following: Yamaha Drums, Zildjian Cymbals, Pro-Mark, Remo, Rhythm Tech, HQ Percussion, and Sennheiser Microphones.

RECORDING CREDITS

Brian Fullen: Drums/Percussion
Michael Rojas: Piano
Timothy Hayden: Piano
Jeff Cox: Acoustic Bass
Pete Huttlinger: Nylon String Guitar

Jeffrey Scot Wills: Saxophones
Dane Bryant: Piano
Dennis Wage: Piano, B3 Organ
Danny O'Lannerghty: Acoustic Bass

Recorded and mixed at The House of Drums. Recording by Brian Fullen. Additional mixing by Randy Thomas at The Radio Ranch, Franklin, TN.

Produced by Brian Fullen (*www.brianfullen.com*)

ACKNOWLEDGEMENTS

Brian would like to thank Jeff Schroedl, Dan Maske, and everyone at Hal Leonard for their limitless patience with this project; Chris, Audra, and Myles for your never-ending support; the Belmont University Library; Dr. Jeff Kirk and the Belmont University School of Music; Joe Testa, John King, John DeChristopher, Kevin Radomski, Matt Connors, Bob Breithaupt, Ed Soph, and Michael Lewis. Special thanks to the incredible musicians who contributed their time, talents, and flexibility.

This book is dedicated to the memory of Elvin Jones.
You have given so much and influenced so many... God bless you.

CONTENTS

PREFACE

Jazz Standards for the Drumset is a text designed to familiarize the drumset student with 12 standard tunes using *Real Book*-type lead sheets and play-along tracks. While encouraging melody memorization, the student will learn concepts that will enhance his/her musical experience. In addition, he/she will learn jazz terminology such as *set-up fills, phrasing, comping, song form*, as well as swing terms and a variety of drumset technique-building exercises and practical applications.

Each lesson in this book will serve to progressively improve the student's ability to understand and perform jazz standards authentically and effectively, as this music requires much more from the drummer than basic timekeeping. However, the musical examples and information merely scratch the surface of this genre. Students are strongly encouraged to expand their knowledge of jazz by researching its history and listening to all of the available resources in the back of this book (see the *Resources* section).

Jazz Standards for the Drumset has been written with the assumption that the student already has a basic knowledge and understanding of music notation as well as the jazz idiom. If deficient in these areas, the author advises studying the following: *Creative Timekeeping for the Contemporary Jazz Drummer* (Hal Leonard – HL006621764), *The Art of Bop Drumming* (Manhattan Music Pub. ISBN 0-89898-890-X), or comparable instruction in these areas.

I hope this book will provide you with some insight into this very important style of music and aid in your future musical endeavors.

–Brian Fullen

ABOUT THE AUDIO

The accompanying audio contains complete arrangements of the 12 jazz standard tunes. Each standard has two versions, one with the drumset (performed by the author), and one without. The tracks with drumset may be listened to for the sake of gaining knowledge of the melodic and harmonic structure of the tune (form). The tracks without drumset are for play-along and performance use. Once learned, the student is encouraged to authentically input their own ideas as they perform with each track.

It is important to note that the performances of these tunes, as they are on the online recordings, are not necessarily definitive to the style, but merely a vehicle for teaching jazz techniques and compositions. In addition, this book and audio provide a means for learning jazz standards, but are not intended to take the place of a live performance.

Track 1, the "comping practice track," should be used when practicing the comping exercises found in Lesson 2. Use the "Loop" function in *PLAYBACK+* for continuous practice. The use of a metronome or the *PLAYBACK+* feature online is also recommended for additional practice at various tempos.

Track 8, the "trading fours practice track," should be used when learning and practicing the exercises found in Lesson 7, "Trading Fours." Again, loop this track for continuous practice. Use of a metronome is also recommended. A versatile, high-quality metronome with headphone plug is strongly recommended.

Audio Track Listing

1   Walking Bass Comping Practice Track

2   "Stompin' at the Savoy" mix (with drumset)
3   "Stompin' at the Savoy" performance track (without drumset)

4   "Things Ain't What They Used to Be" mix (with drumset)
5   "Things Ain't What They Used to Be" performance track (without drumset)

6   "All of Me" mix (with drumset)
7   "All of Me" performance track (without drumset)

8   "Trading Fours Practice Track" performance track (without drumset)

9   "Take the 'A' Train" mix (with drumset)
10   "Take the 'A' Train" performance track (without drumset)

11   "Satin Doll" mix (with drumset)
12   "Satin Doll" performance track (without drumset)

13   "Don't Get Around Much Anymore" mix (with drumset)
14   "Don't Get Around Much Anymore" performance track (without drumset)

15   "Body and Soul" mix (with drumset)
16   "Body and Soul" performance track (without drumset)

17   "Four" mix (with drumset)
18   "Four" performance track (without drumset)

19   "Bluesette" mix (with drumset)
20   "Bluesette" performance track (without drumset)

21   "The Girl from Ipanema" mix (with drumset)
22   "The Girl from Ipanema" performance track (without drumset)

23   "St. Thomas" mix (with drumset)
24   "St. Thomas" performance track (without drumset)

25   "Mercy, Mercy, Mercy" mix (with drumset)
26   "Mercy, Mercy, Mercy" performance track (without drumset)

INTRODUCTION

Jazz: an infinite and enduring form of musical expression.

Referred to as the essence of all popular music, jazz has played a vast cultural role throughout the world. Now 100 years in the making, America's indigenous music is the common thread through which all contemporary popular music is birthed, leaving its eternal imprint on American history. From its inception, jazz has offered musical creativity and evolution, paralleling developing life throughout the twentieth century and beyond.

To name artists and composers such as Duke Ellington, Louis Armstrong, "King" Oliver, Count Basie, Bix Beiderbecke, James P. Johnson, Miles Davis, Benny Carter, John Coltrane, Ornette Coleman, Charlie Parker, Dizzy Gillespie, Charles Mingus, Thelonious Monk, Roy Eldridge, Benny Goodman, Coleman Hawkins, Earl Hines, Bill Evans, Sonny Rollins, Ella Fitzgerald, Billie Holiday, Stan Getz, Chick Corea, Joe Zawinul, and Herbie Hancock, is to incredibly name but a few of the jazz innovators who have contributed pivotal compositions and legendary performances.

Drummers such as Jo Jones, Max Roach, Art Blakey, Sid Catlett, Baby Dodds, Chick Webb, Gene Krupa, Buddy Rich, Philly Joe Jones, Elvin Jones, Roy Haynes, and Tony Williams, are among the countless drummers who have performed with many of these great artists and have equally contributed to the evolution and development of America's music. Please see the *Jazz Legends and Notable Drummers* section of this book for a listing of important jazz drummers.

As a result, percussion instructors and educators at major universities across the country have customized and taught jazz concepts for many years. The reason: jazz drumming techniques are the quintessential way to teach drumset students how to be great musicians, no matter what style of music they ultimately pursue. Concepts such as composition, improvisation, musical interplay, creativity, finesse, tonality, melody, and harmony become ingrained in their musical senses.

Among the best ways to explore these jazz drumming concepts is through the use of classic jazz standard compositions. *Jazz Standards for Drumset* provides drummers with an excellent play-along resource to learn, memorize, and perform these important compositions.

JAZZ TERMINOLOGY

The following is a partial list of standard terms and phrases jazz musicians use to communicate musically with one another. Louis Armstrong is largely responsible for creating or popularizing much of the musical slang. While all of these terms are used in the jazz idiom, many have also progressed into other styles of music. For more information, check out *The New Grove Dictionary of Jazz*.

AABA • A common 32-bar song form. Each of the four segments are generally eight bars in length. The first musical theme (A) is repeated (A), followed by a second musical theme (B), returning to the first theme (A).

Arrangement • An adaptation or reworking of a composition for other instruments to be used in a specific performance.

Antiphonal • Call and response, or question and answer.

Backbeat • The drummer's strong accent of beats 2 and 4, commonly striking the snare drum; also, a general reference to beats 2 and 4 in a 4/4 composition.

Ballad • A romantic or sentimental composition generally at a medium to slow tempo, and generally ranging from 60 to 120 beats per minute.

Beat • The succession of basic metrical units of rhythm; the pulse.

Blues • A style of music evolved from Southern African-American culture featuring a standard length of 12 bars, with a lyric comprised of a four-bar question, then repeated, and a four-bar answer.

Break • When the ensemble or rhythm section stops playing and a soloist or instrument continues, introducing a new section of music.

Bridge • The B section or transitional passage connecting two segments of a composition.

Changes • The chord progression that defines the harmonic structure of a jazz composition.

Chorus • One complete time through the song form.

Comping • Improvised, compositional *accompaniment* of a rhythm section instrument to a soloist in a jazz ensemble; to musically *complement* a soloist; the interplay between the bass drum and snare drum in the jazz idiom.

Double Time • A tempo that is double the original tempo or pace of a composition—although, at times, the chord progression remains at the original rate.

Downbeat • The first beat of a measure or bar; each beat of a measure.

Four-Feel • Refers to the emphasis of all four beats in a 4/4 measure, generally accentuated by a walking bass pattern and jazz ride cymbal, resulting in a quarter-note pulse.

Head • The melody of a jazz composition.

Head Arrangement • The performance of a jazz piece that is improvised on the spot and not written down.

Laid-Back • The rhythmic feeling of playing the pulse slightly behind the actual metronomic placement of the beat.

Lead Sheet • A musical chart or manuscript containing only the melody and harmonic structure of a composition.

Medium Swing • Generally refers to the tempo and musical style of a jazz composition, with a triplet feel, ranging from 120 to 200 beats per minute.

Melody • A rhythmically organized arrangement of single notes that define the primary shape or idea of a composition.

Meter • The specific rhythm determined by the number of beats and time value assigned to each note in a measure.

Off Beat • A rhythm that is placed somewhere in the measure other than on the downbeat.

On Top • The rhythmic feeling of playing the pulse slightly ahead of the actual metronomic placement of the beat.

Out Chorus • The final chorus (one complete time through the form) of a jazz performance.

Phrase • A musical passage or segment, often consisting of equal measures, forming part of a larger, complete unit.

Polyrhythmic • The simultaneous use of contrasting rhythms.

Real Book • The commonly used collection of jazz standards in lead sheet form (note: every musician desiring to play jazz should own one!).

Rhythm • The varying patterns and motions of musical movement through metronomic time.

Rhythm Section • The part of the jazz ensemble that consists of any combination of drums, bass, piano, guitar, and vibes, whose basic role is to provide the rhythmic and harmonic accompaniment to the ensemble.

Riff • A repeated melodic phrase.

Setup Fill • The rhythmic and often syncopated pattern or fill a drummer plays around the drumset just before an accented rhythmic figure, simultaneously played by the ensemble.

Solo • The improvisational performance by a single jazz instrumentalist or vocalist.

Solo Chorus • A jazz instrumentalist improvises a solo one complete time through the song form.

Stomp • Refers to a *swinging performance* of a composition; a dance involving a rhythmical, heavy step.

Stop Time • Short specific rhythms generally played by the rhythm section, accentuating specific parts of the musical segment.

Straight Ahead • The performance of a composition within the typical 4/4-time jazz format.

Tag • The extended ending of a composition that repeats a portion of the closing theme or idea, generally four or eight bars in length.

Tempo • Refers to the *beats per minute* rate at which the speed or pulse of a composition is played (example: ♩ = 120).

Timbre • The characteristic sound or tone color of a vocalist, instrument, or group of instruments.

Trading Fours • Most commonly referred to as the alternating of four-bar improvisational segments between solo instrumentalists and the drummer.

Tutti • A passage of ensemble music intended to be executed by all the instrumentalists simultaneously, with rhythm section accompaniment.

Two-Feel • Refers to the alternating emphasis of the first and third beats of the 4/4 measure, by the rhythm section, resulting in a half-note pulse.

"Up" or Uptempo Swing • Generally refers to the tempo and musical style of a jazz composition, most likely bebop, with a triplet feel, ranging from 200 to 300 beats per minute.

Vamp • A continuous repeating section of a tune (often indefinite), which generally accompanies an improvised solo.

THE JAZZ SETUP

DRUMS

The jazz drumset traditionally consists of a small bass drum, snare drum, one mounted tom, and one floor tom, although many variations of this setup are widely used today.

A variety of drumhead choices are available. Most jazz drummers choose heads that resemble the sound and feel of calfskin heads, since plastic heads didn't become commonly used until the 1960s. Consult your local drum dealer and experiment to find the right sound for your musical needs.

The **bass drum** is generally 18 to 20 inches in diameter, with little or no muffling, tuned to a high enough pitch to retain the resonant qualities of the drum. Unlike rock styles where the bass drum is used as a foundational instrument, the jazz bass drum is most often used as an extension of the hands. However, if the bass drum becomes too loud, it can disrupt the flow and authenticity of the jazz time feel. Practice "feathering" (playing softly) the bass drum, only accenting specific rhythmic figures. Play the bass drum with your heel down, allowing the (felt) beater to quickly rebound off the head for resonance, avoiding "burying the beater" (although this has become more common).

The **snare drum** is generally 14 inches in diameter and 5 1/2 inches in depth, although a variety of sizes are available. Light muffling may be used to reduce unwanted resonance, but is not always recommended. Instead, experiment with tuning out any unwanted overtones, making sure the drum is in tune with itself. The sound you end up with (after tuning) should give you a crisp, full tone and resonance. After that, muffle accordingly if desired.

The **mounted** and **floor toms** are generally 12 and 14 inches in diameter, respectively. They are sometimes tuned to a higher pitch, and the tuning should always help provide a warm, resonant tone, blending with the bass drum and snare drum. Again, experiment with the different possibilities and seek further guidance, if needed.

CYMBALS

The jazz ride cymbal is generally 20 or 22 inches in diameter. A dry, light, or medium light cymbal is most suitable in that it provides the appropriate resonance and stick definition required to play a flowing jazz time pattern, without becoming too "washy." Heavier ride cymbals, such as rock cymbals are inappropriate and tend to sound short and fragmented. Dark, dry sounding ride cymbals are recommended, such as the Zildjian K series. It is also recommended that you use at least two ride cymbals in your jazz setup. Experiment!

STICKS

Choose a versatile stick that works well for you in this style of music. Remember, a rock stick or one that is very heavy in the shoulder may overwork the ride cymbal, disrupting the definition and flow. "Back weighted" sticks provide a nice rebound off the ride, while retaining the necessary definition. Changing sticks for every style of music you play can become arduous and expensive. So, try and find one or two stick models that provide what you need. The Pro-Mark "FunkBat" is recommended and very versatile.

BRUSHES

A variety of brushes are available from several manufacturers. Wire and plastic brushes; retractable, wooden handles; varied thickness; and flexibility of wire and strands also provide for many options. Wire brushes provide brighter cymbal and snare tones, while plastic brushes are more durable for louder playing. However, plastic brushes generally don't provide as much cymbal definition as wire. The Pro-Mark Accent Brush is a wood-handled durable wire brush with great flexibility and cymbal definition. Choose a brush that suits your playing style and volume needs.

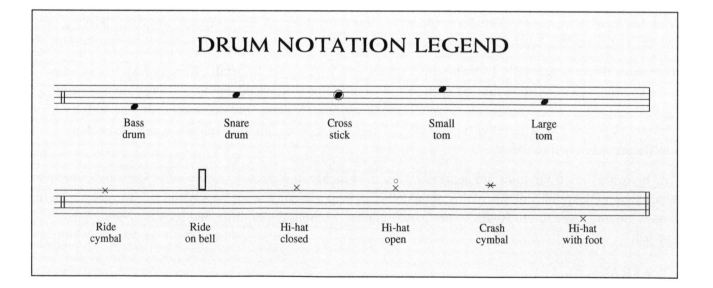

1 RIDE CYMBAL BASICS

A Brief History

Rock beats are generally built from the "bottom up," with the bass drum and snare drum defining the pulse. Cymbals are then used as "icing" to propel, or slightly alter the rock feel with various eighth or sixteenth notes. Jazz drumming styles are just the opposite. In jazz, the defining rhythmic pulse often comes from the swing pattern played on the ride cymbal. The bass drum and snare drum are then used to complement the ride cymbal. Interestingly, the jazz pattern originated on the snare drum in the early days of ragtime. Before making its way to the ride cymbal in the 1940s, however, the jazz rhythm evolved to the hi-hat (or sock cymbal). Hi-hat master Jo Jones was so innovative that Max Roach later recorded a hi-hat solo called "Mr. Jo's Hi-Hat," in recognition of Jo's influence.

During World War II, the government had imposed a tax on public dancing, which in turn initiated the demise of the big bands. Clubs were closing, which meant the large dance bands were losing money and were unable to work. Jazz quartets, quintets, and trios quickly emerged, making musical changes inevitable. As drummers began to play more freely, a new style of jazz drumming naturally evolved and the primary method of keeping time shifted from the bass drum to the cymbal. Avedis Zildjian responded by making larger cymbals called "bounces" or "rides." Bop cymbals, introduced in the late 1940s, were described as "eighteen through twenty-four inches in diameter" and were designed to produce the "pingy" tones associated with the new, more modern jazz drumming style.

A jazz drummer's unique touch on the ride cymbal is the cornerstone on which jazz timekeeping is built. Listening to drummers such as Jo Jones, Kenny Clarke, Louie Bellson, Max Roach, Buddy Rich, Philly Joe Jones, Elvin Jones, Shelly Manne, Roy Haynes, Tony Williams, Jack DeJohnette, Mel Lewis, Steve Smith, and Peter Erskine, among many others, will help to provide a diverse understanding of ride cymbal feel and techniques. (Check out the *Resources* section of this book for more information.)

Motions and Timekeeping

When playing the ride cymbal, a full cymbal tone is created by maintaining a relaxed and consistent arm motion. This consistent motion also causes equal distances (or spaces) in between each stroke, which helps maintain a steady tempo. Faster tempos require less space/distance between notes, while slower tempos require more space. Steve Smith briefly discusses this technique in his DVD *Drumset Technique/History of the U.S. Beat*, Disk 1, Chapter 68.

As an example of equal distances, try bouncing a tennis ball from approximately 48" above the ground and catching it at the same place. If the perfect amount of energy is consistently put into each ball each time it is thrown to the ground, it naturally and effortlessly rebounds right back to your hand. If the ball is bounced at an angle, it rebounds in the opposite direction. Or, if too little or too much energy is used, the ball rebounds improperly. Much is the same with the tip of the drumstick when striking the ride cymbal.

Play the ride cymbal as you normally would. As you continue playing, increase the distance between the tip of your drumstick and the ride cymbal to approximately 6"–12" above the cymbal. After each strike of the cymbal, allow the tip of the stick to naturally rebound back to this position, just like a tennis ball. This is referred to as a "full stroke." The rebound of the drumstick is often taken for granted in other styles of music, but becomes evident when playing jazz. Be sure to maintain a relaxed, consistent motion.

Technique

Developing a jazz ride cymbal technique takes practice, and will become more comfortable as you play and experiment with various sounds and patterns. Jazz drummers have various ways to achieve a great sound on the ride cymbal. Pay close attention to the techniques used by your favorite jazz drummers and study them.

The following is a technique that will help you get started:

There are four basic elbow positions when playing the jazz ride pattern (see photos 1–8). These movements subdivide the quarter-note pulse into eighths. Consistently using this motion will help you achieve a full cymbal sound, while keeping a steady tempo. Remember, allow the stick to consistently rebound off the ride cymbal!

See example A. The first measure in this example shows the jazz ride pattern with an eighth-note subdivision underneath. The second measure shows the position of the elbow in relation to each subdivided eighth note. This should be a smooth arm motion when playing the jazz ride pattern. With practice, it will become second nature. Notice how much better the ride cymbal sounds, and how much easier it is to play steady time. Practice fluid motion!!

Start with a straight eighth-note subdivision:

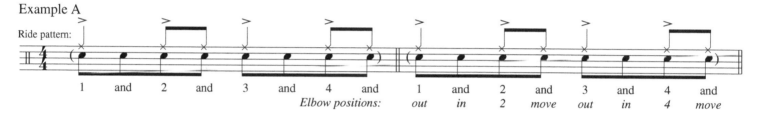

Example A

Start with the elbow out, slightly away from the body, striking the cymbal on beat 1 (photo 1). On the "and" of beat 1, quickly move the elbow in towards the body while raising the top of the stick 6–12 inches straight up (photo 2). Strike the cymbal on beat 2, allowing the stick tip to rebound off the cymbal (photo 3). Immediately move the elbow towards the out position on the "and" of beat 2 (photo 4).

Beat 3: Again, the elbow should be in the out position (photo 5). On the "and" of beat 3, quickly move the elbow in towards the body while raising the tip of the stick 6–12 inches straight up (photo 6). Strike the cymbal on beat 4, again allowing the stick tip to rebound off the ride cymbal (photo 7). Move the elbow towards the out position on the "and" of beat 4 (photo 8). Repeat the process several times slowly, working on smooth motions. Once comfortable, increase the tempo.

Remember, the faster the tempo, the smaller the motions; the slower the tempo, the bigger the motions. This ensures that the proper amount of space is used in between each note, and keeps the unnecessary movements to a minimum.

Photo 1

Photo 2

Photo 3

Photo 4   Photo 5   Photo 6

Photo 7   Photo 8

The Jazz Time Pattern

The standard swing ride cymbal pattern is found in example B. Although it is commonly played this way (with a triplet eighth-note feel), it is often notated using eighth notes as in example C, referred to as "swing eighths."

Example B   Example C
                                              Swing eighths

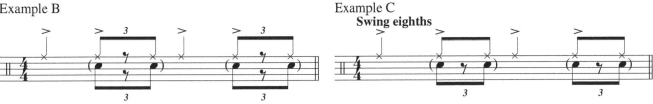

Example C is played with the same triplet feel as example B. The eighth notes are referred to as "swing eighths."

The Quarter-Note Pulse

It is important to preserve the quarter-note pulse when playing swing. This steady quarter-note pulse emulates the walking bass line and keeps the "four-feel" moving in a forward motion (example D). The over accenting of beats 1 and 3, or the upbeat of beats 2 and 4, often make the time feel unsettled, or erratic (see examples E and F).

Example D

For a greater understanding of the jazz ride pattern, the book *Creative Timekeeping for the Contemporary Jazz Drummer* by Rick Mattingly is suggested.

Accenting beats 1 and 3 feels awkward when playing swing. For most rock drummers, this is a common mistake when attempting to play swing.

Example E

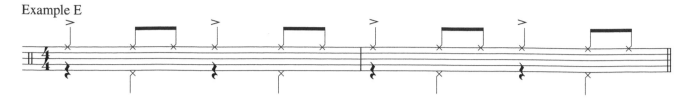

Accenting the "upbeats" is not an uncommon practice among jazz drummers. However, unless perfected, this tends to disrupt the time flow.

Example F

Summary

- Maintain a relaxed and consistent motion in the arms, wrist, and fingers.

- Put energy into each stroke, allowing the stick to perfectly rebound 6–12 inches.

- Evenly space each note, keeping the tempo steady.

- Faster tempos, less space; slower tempos, more space between each note.

- Maintain an even, quarter-note pulse.

- Think triplet subdivision of each quarter note.

- Pull sound out of the drums and cymbals with rebound strokes.

- Be creative and make music.

2 COMPING

Definition

Comping is to "rhythmically accompany" a jazz soloist using interplay around the drumset—primarily the bass drum and snare drum. As "bebop" developed, innovative drummers such as Kenny Clarke and Max Roach were playing more syncopated rhythms on the drumset, and shifting the method of timekeeping from the bass drum to the ride cymbal. Small groups were on the rise, which gave drummers the freedom to react musically to each soloist. Today, the musical concept of "comping" has become standard when playing jazz. This lesson will take you through a series of coordination exercises and patterns to help you develop this technique.

RIDE CYMBAL/HI-HAT JAZZ TIME PATTERN

Reminder: This first, straight eighth jazz notation actually *sounds* like the second, triplet time pattern below.

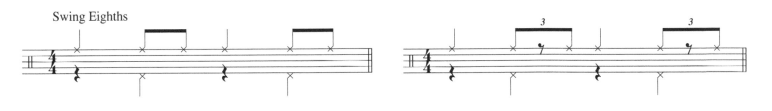

Beginning Coordination Exercises

TRACK 1
Walking Bass/Comping
Practice Track

Quarter Notes

Using track 1, ♩ = 122, play and repeat the following coordination exercises on the bass drum and snare drum as indicated, while playing the above jazz time pattern with the ride cymbal and hi-hat (examples 1–4 show both patterns played at the same time). Loop track 1 for continuous practice.

Examples: ♩ = **100-200** (suggested tempo range)

Continue playing the following quarter-note coordination exercises 5–16 in the same way. The ride cymbal/hi-hat jazz time pattern is not notated here, but should be played along with each example. The snare and bass drum notation will be specifically indicated for each exercise and will continue as such throughout this section of the book.

Play each exercise a minimum of sixteen times using track 1, continuing to the next exercise without stopping. Once accomplished, use a metronome or *PLAYBACK+* and increase or decrease the tempo 10–20 beats per minute to practice at a variety of tempos.

Eighth Notes

Continue using track 1 to play the following eighth-note coordination exercises in the bass drum and snare drum as indicated. Remember to add the ride cymbal/hi-hat jazz time pattern and loop this track for continuous practice. Play the snare drum at a volume equal to or less than the ride cymbal.

Upbeats – Snare Drum

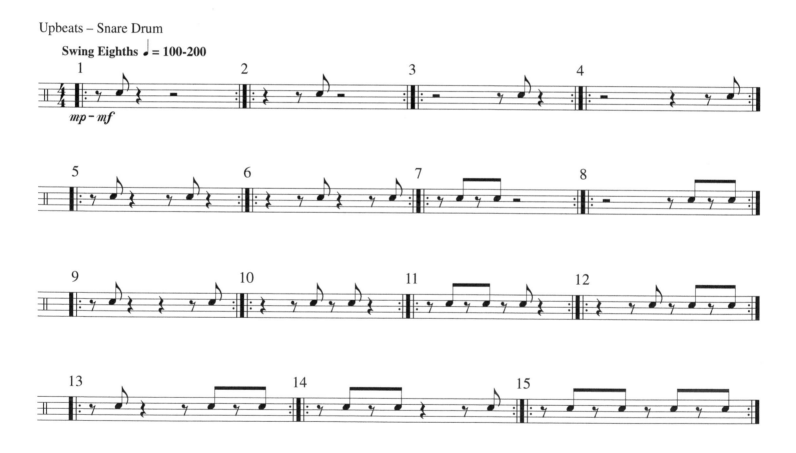

Play each exercise a minimum of sixteen times, continuing to the next exercise without stopping. Use a metronome or *PLAYBACK+* to increase or decrease the tempo at least 10–20 beats per minute and repeat the process. Play the bass drum at a volume equal to or less than that of the ride cymbal.

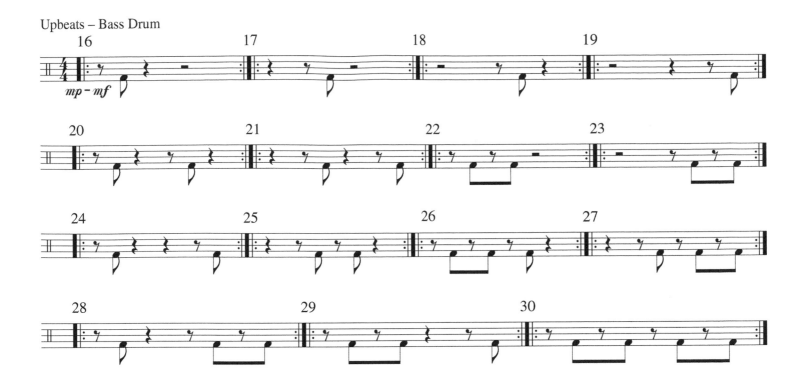

Combination Patterns

Play as before using track 1 or a metronome for continued practice.

One-Bar Phrases

$\quad \downarrow = 100\text{-}200$

Two-Bar Phrases

Paradiddles and Inversions

Musical Studies: Phrase Development

The following studies focus on comping ideas and phrase development. By combining the quarter notes and eighth notes from the previous exercises, one-bar musical phrases can be created. Completion of this study will aid you in the development of your own comping phrases, which should include a musical idea or theme like the ones below. In performance, listening and reacting to a soloist or melody figure will motivate musical ideas. Note: When playing jazz, be sure *not* to over-emphasize beat 1 with the bass drum.

Using track 1 or a metronome, play the following swing eighth-note studies in the same way as the Beginning Coordination Exercises (as in examples 1–4).

ONE-BAR MUSICAL PHRASES

One-Bar Musical Phrases

Continue examples 5–32 as above. Once you've mastered these exercises, try substituting the bass drum rhythm with the hi-hat.

Paradiddles and Inversions

TWO-BAR MUSICAL PHRASES

"Comping is the spontaneous reaction to a soloist or rhythmic figure, using syncopated bass drum and snare drum patterns."

Each of the following two-bar comping phrases have a musical idea or theme (as before). After completing this study, try creating and developing your own musical phrases while comping. Be sure to maintain a smooth, consistent, swinging ride cymbal pattern, and be aware *not* to overemphasize beat 1 with the bass drum.

Swing Eighths ♩ = 100-200

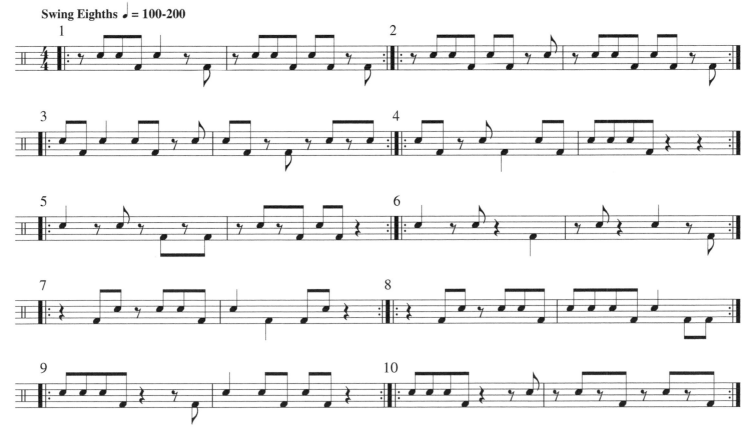

FOUR-BAR MUSICAL PHRASES

The following study gives you an example of how to take a four-bar musical theme or idea (exercise 1 below) and develop it with variations (2–8). The ride cymbal and hi-hat should play a steady jazz time pattern as before, while the musical theme (or melody) is played in the bass drum and snare drum. Once you've mastered these exercises, substitute the bass drum rhythms with the hi-hat. Use track 1 or a metronome for continuous practice.

Try writing your own four-bar musical phrases and expanding them with several variations! Remember to play musically; it is not necessary to overplay. As you develop your own phrases, try starting the variation patterns on a subsequent beat or inserting bars of time to create odd phrases.

Four-bar musical theme or main idea

Progressive variations of the main musical theme

Advanced Coordination Exercises

TRIPLETS

Play the following eighth-note triplet exercises with the jazz time pattern as before. These triplet patterns offer more of a challenge than the earlier eighth-note figures. If you are having difficulty executing these patterns, try working them out slowly (see example below).

> Set your metronome to ♩ = 60. First, play the snare drum/bass drum pattern alone (see exercise A). Once you're comfortable and playing the pattern consistently, add the hi-hat on beats 2 and 4 (exercise B). Take note as to whether the hi-hat is playing exactly with the bass drum or snare drum, and line them up (in this case, the bass drum). Finally, add the ride cymbal (exercise C). Again, be sure to accurately line up the triplets in the bass drum and snare drum with the ride cymbal.

This approach to working out an exercise will solidify the relationship between your bass drum and snare drum, and give you a greater understanding of how the pattern "fits" together. Before long, you will be able to play each pattern effortlessly without stopping to work them out.

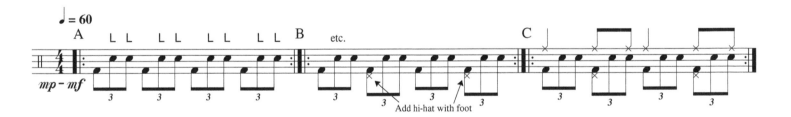

Play exercises 1–16 as above, slowly working out each pattern as needed. For further study of comping and triplets, the following books are highly recommended:

*   *Creative Timekeeping for the Contemporary Jazz Drummer* by Rick Mattingly (Hal Leonard)
*   *The Art of Bop Drumming* by John Riley (Manhattan Music Publications)
*   *Advanced Techniques for the Modern Drummer* by Jim Chapin

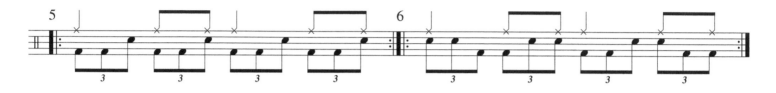

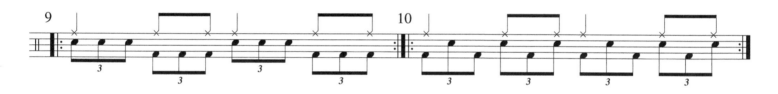

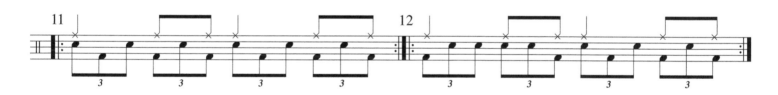

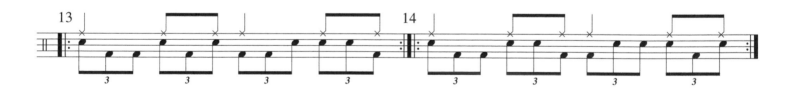

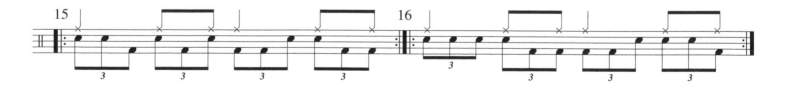

3 OUTLINING THE MELODY

Definition

To "outline the melody" is to musically accent (or highlight) various notes and rhythms of the melody using the drumset. This is generally motivated by how the drummer hears and responds to the interpretation of a melody, performed by an instrumentalist or a singer.

Application

As you listen to the long and short tones of a melodic phrase, try matching those long and short tones with your drumset. For example, strike a crash cymbal and let it ring for a specific amount of time, such as two or four beats, then dampen. The cymbals can be used to musically mimic long and short tones of the melody. Striking the snare drum or bass drum along with the ride or crash cymbal creates an "accented" long or short tone. Try using a variety of crash cymbals and sizes. (Note: As in rock styles, accenting the different sections of a jazz arrangement with the crash cymbal is acceptable; however, crashing too loudly may overpower the melody. As an alternative, try digging into the ride cymbal with the shoulder of your drumstick. This creates a nice cymbal accent without overpowering the ensemble. See example below.) Striking the snare or bass drum by itself makes a short tone.

Experiment by playing each drum and cymbal around your drumset to determine the long and short tones you can create, and then apply them in any musical setting. Listening to great jazz recordings will help you in this process.

In the A section of "Stompin' at the Savoy" (track 2), the main melody revolves around two long notes. In example 1 below, see how the drums reflect these two long notes with snare drum/cymbal, bass drum/ cymbal combinations, while lightly comping around the counter-melody on the snare.

Example 1

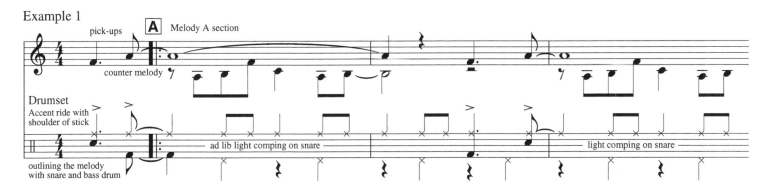

Try outlining the melody in the 7th and 8th bars of the B section (or bridge). This creates a nice musical moment at the end of this melodic phrase. Stay musical and experiment! See example 2.

Example 2

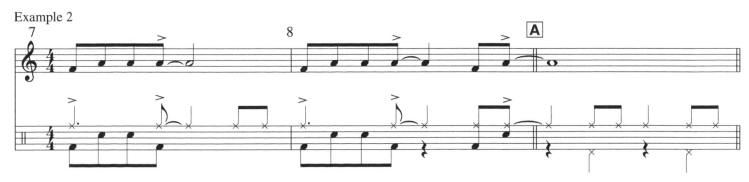

Play Along: "Stompin' at the Savoy"

Benny Goodman/Chick Webb/Edgar Sampson

Synopsis

A Few Recommended Recordings

- *Ultimate Clifford Brown,* Verve/PolyGram, 1998
  Personnel (1954): Max Roach, drums; George Morrow, bass;
  Richie Powell, piano; Harold Land, tenor sax; Clifford Brown, trumpet
- *The Immortal Benny Goodman: The Big Bands* (two-CD set)
- *Greatest Swing: Golden Greats,* various artists (three-CD set)

Tune Form and Analysis

The form of this tune is the classic 32-bar or AABA. Each of the four segments are eight bars in length. The first eight-bar musical theme (A) repeats, then releases to the second theme (B), or bridge, returning to the final (A) section.

The A section of this tune features a melody and counter-melody. Early Benny Goodman big band versions featured the horn section playing the main melody while the saxophone answered with the counter-melody—a somewhat typical approach during the swing era. Clifford Brown's small group arrangement features Clifford playing the main melody on trumpet while Harold Land answers with the counter-melody on the tenor saxophone. Note: On this recording, Max Roach plays a two-chorus (64-bar) drum solo that mirrors the melody, while keeping the tempo steady and the AABA form intact!

Play-Along Track Arrangement

This arrangement of "Stompin' at the Savoy" (track 2) is very straightforward. Be aware that the melody plays two pickup notes starting on beat 3 prior to the first downbeat, which will affect the count-off (see example). The head (melody) plays one time through and stops at the end of the 30th bar, giving the soloist measures 31 and 32 to begin soloing (a common practice when playing jazz standards). There is only one solo chorus, which is split between the saxophone (A-A, 16 bars) and piano (B-A, 16 bars). The head is then played one final time, again ending rhythmically in the 30th measure.

Approach

Understanding the musical style of the tune you are playing is very helpful. "Stompin' at the Savoy" was written during the swing era, when drummers generally played steady quarter-note time. However, the emergence of the small combos gave drummers the freedom and liberation to play syncopated figures in support of the melody and soloists.

Listen closely to track 2. This recording features the saxophone playing the melody, while the piano answers with the counter-melody. In the small group setting, it is acceptable to play syncopated musical figures around the melody and solos. Memorizing the tune form and melody aids in this musical interaction! However, be careful not to overplay or overshadow the melodic phrase.

Remember, the jazz time feel is more about the ride cymbal than the bass drum and snare drum. Allow the stick to rebound nicely off the ride cymbal, while maintaining consistency in your sound and subdivisions. Approach this track with an easy, steady four-feel, outlining the melody in spots, and comping lightly with the snare drum and bass drum when appropriate.

Countoff Examples:

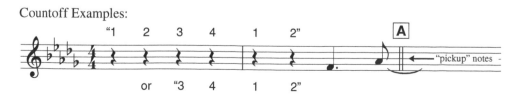

STOMPIN' AT THE SAVOY

-BENNY GOODMAN/EDGAR SAMPSON/CHICK WEBB

TRACK 2
with drumset

TRACK 3
without drumset

SETUP FILLS

Definition

A setup fill is the rhythmic and often syncopated drum fill a drummer plays around the drumset in preparation of an accented rhythmic figure, played by the ensemble or band.

Application

Setup drum fills are played in virtually any style of music, such as jazz, rock, Latin, country, etc., and are used to "set up" and support rhythmic ensemble figures in a given arrangement. Setup fills can also be used to build or reduce dynamic intensity throughout a song or during a solo chorus. They range from simple and understated to complex and featured.

There are many creative ways to utilize setup fills. For the purpose of this lesson, we will focus primarily on the setup and support of rhythmic ensemble figures.

Notice the rhythmic figure in measure 2 of example 1. This notation indicates the accented rhythm played by the entire band or ensemble. A drum fill is played within the first three beats of measure 2, "setting up" the accented ensemble figure.

When performing with a group, the drummer should look ahead to see the upcoming ensemble figure, which is to be accented on the "and" or "upbeat" of beats 3 and 4. Quickly, he/she calculates that beats 1, 2, and 3 (before the figure), are available for playing a tasty drum fill, "setting up" the ensemble figure.

Example 1

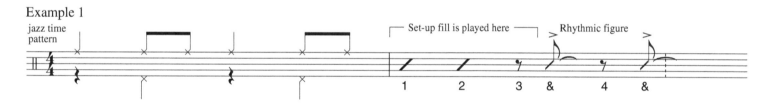

In the illustrated examples below (2 and 3), the drum fill "sets up" the ensemble figure. Example 2 is a short, understated fill, while example 3 is a longer, more pronounced fill. Either one works well.

After playing a setup fill, the drummer then supports (accents) the ensemble figure. Possibilities include the use of a bass drum and crash cymbal, or snare drum and crash cymbal, played simultaneously.

Example 2   Example 3

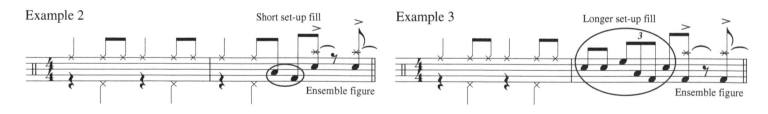

Development: Snare Drum

Typically, a setup fill may last one to four beats prior to the ensemble figure. In the following examples A–E, the second measure is divided using eighth notes on the snare drum. Each subsequent example (B-E) shows the snare drum beginning the fill a half-beat later than the one before it. This illustrates the progression from a three-beat drum fill to a one-beat drum fill.

(Understanding musical math and how a measure can be divided is essential. Seek out private music instruction, if needed.)

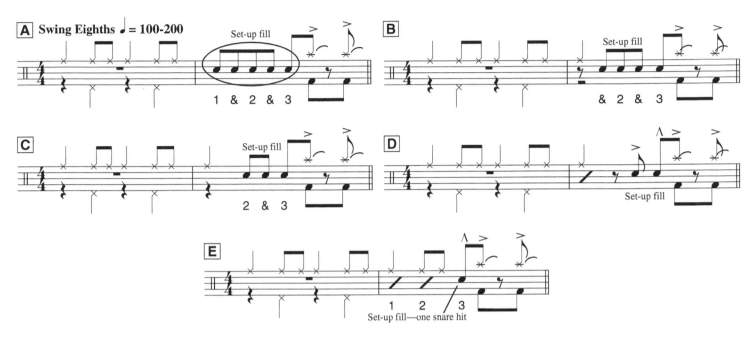

Development: Around the Toms

Continue this lesson by moving each eighth-note fill around the drumset. When you are comfortable, try other rhythms, such as triplets, sixteenth notes, etc. Experiment with your own fills! Note: When playing a drum fill, always keep the beat steady and remember where you are in each measure. The other musicians you are playing with trust you to do this!

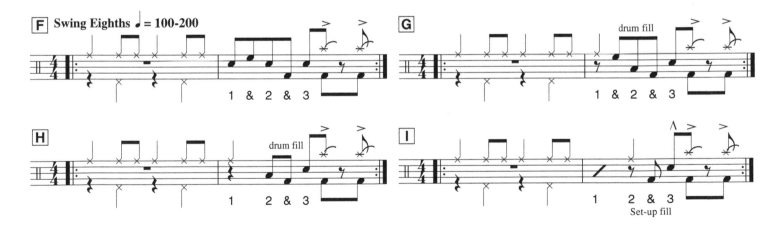

Multiple Setup Fills

Many ensemble figures require multiple drum fills. Example 4 illustrates where each drum fill might be placed when reading multiple rhythms. The idea is to set up and support each figure, while maintaining a smooth transition through the measure.

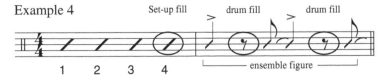

Example 4

Exercises J–M show an example of how to play multiple fills through the ensemble figure in example 4. Notice how the snare drum plays in between and around the rhythmic figure in exercise J. After playing through each exercise, try your own fills and be creative! Remember to keep the tempo steady and divide each measure evenly.

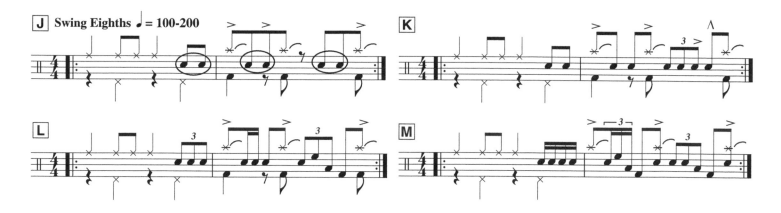

Long and Short Tones

Rhythmic figures are often notated as "long" or "short"; this is called "articulation." The figure in example 5 indicates long, accented tones, which may require a bass drum and cymbal crash. The same figure in example 6 indicates short, accented tones, such as the use of a snare drum struck by itself *without* a crash cymbal. Spend time striking each drum and cymbal to determine the long and short tones of your drumset. Then apply those sounds to the articulations you hear when performing with other instrumentalists, and each play-along track.

Example 5

Example 6

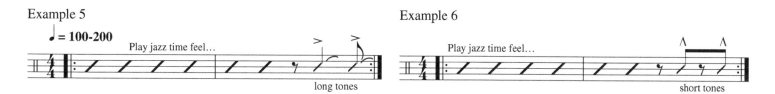

EXERCISES

You now understand that a drum fill being played prior to an ensemble figure can be referred to as a "setup fill." As you are listening to your favorite drummers, notice the fills being played and emulate what you hear. Then, try and add these fills to your drumming vocabulary!

Practice playing drum fills around the rhythmic figures below. It is probable that the notation you will see on a drum chart looks similar to these. However, there are many possibilities. Be sure to keep the tempo steady and play fills that are appropriate. Experiment, be musical, and have fun!

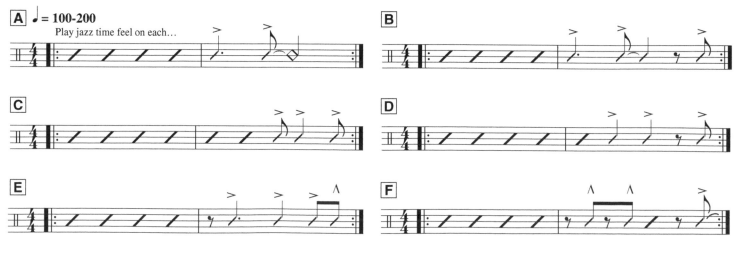

5 THE SHUFFLE

Definition

A shuffle generally has a "walking" four-feel with constant swing eighths throughout the measure, and should be played on the "backside" of the beat—not rushed. The bass player will also play four quarter notes to the measure. Shuffles are very common in blues music, a kind of American music derived from emotional spirituals and work songs. Blues can be heard in areas such as Memphis, Chicago, Austin, and St. Louis, among others. Spend time listening to recordings so you can acquire a sense of this characteristic sound.

Application

When playing the shuffle, create a "pocket" by keeping the swing eighths constant. The soft shuffle strokes should all remain steady and identical in volume, accenting only the backbeat strokes on beats 2 and 4. This dynamic consistency is vital to playing a great shuffle! Additionally, only play fills when needed or to set up a rhythmic figure, otherwise settle into a solid groove and stay there. Dig into the bass drum, and put a little "grease" on your feel. Listen to track 4 for an example.

Shuffle Examples

Both hands playing the shuffle simultaneously is often referred to as a "double shuffle" (see example 2). Play through each example below at varying tempos.

FOUR-FEEL SHUFFLES

Simplified variation of example 3 with open/closed hi-hat pattern:

Double shuffle variation of example 2 with quarter notes on ride cymbal:

Variation of example 4 with open/closed hi-hat pattern:

Simplified variation of example 7

TWO-FEEL SHUFFLES

Play Along: "Things Ain't What They Used to Be"

Mercer Ellington

Synopsis

A Few Recommended Recordings

- Duke Ellington, *Live at the Blue Note* (recorded August, 1959)

- *Stuff Smith, Dizzy Gillespie, Oscar Peterson* (recorded March 1957)
  Personnel: Stuff Smith, violin; Oscar Peterson, piano; Barney Kessel, guitar; Ray Brown, bass; Alvin Stoller, drums

- Gene Harris, *The Gene Harris Trio Plus One* (recorded live, November/December, 1985)
  Personnel: Gene Harris, piano; Ray Brown, bass; Mickey Roker, drums; Stanley Turrentine, tenor sax

Tune Form and Analysis

This is a 12-bar blues form, made up of two different 12-bar sections. The first twelve bars, section A, is the main theme; the beginning two-bar phrase is repeated three times before releasing into the final phrase. This is a common practice with blues form. The second twelve bars, section B, is referred to as a "shout chorus," which is the pinnacle of the big band chart.

In big band style, the "shout chorus" figure was often played in unison by the remaining horn players, as the soloist continued to wail over the top! This technique was quite exciting and would often work the audience into a frenzy!

Play-Along Track Arrangement

Four beats of triplets on the floor tom and snare drum set up the beginning of the tune, which starts with the melody. The head is played through one complete time (AB), followed by one complete saxophone solo chorus (24 bars). The piano then solos for an additional chorus, followed by the A section of the melody only. The last four bars of this final A section are tagged, twice. The piano then leads the band into a big finish, with a typical blues ending.

Approach

Listen to track 4. The main shuffle patterns to be played are found in examples A and B. Try playing example C at the beginning of each solo chorus for dynamic contrast. The idea is to play and maintain a steady, constant "four-feel" shuffle groove throughout, only playing fills when needed. Snapping beats 2 and 4 on the snare drum will help create a deep pocket. Use soft-to-loud dynamics to build each solo, keeping the tempo steady in the process. Lay back, dig in, and groove hard!

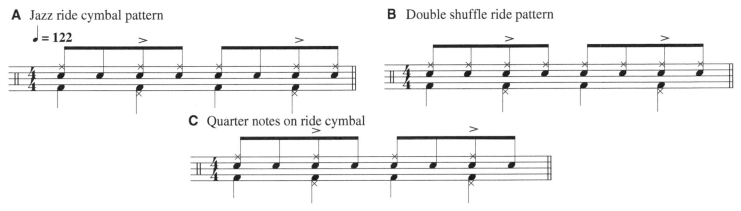

The section B shout chorus has a rhythmic figure that should be supported by the drummer. Play a setup fill over the first two beats of measures 1 and 3 prior to the "and" of beat 2, which should be accented by the drums. Listen to track 4 for an example.

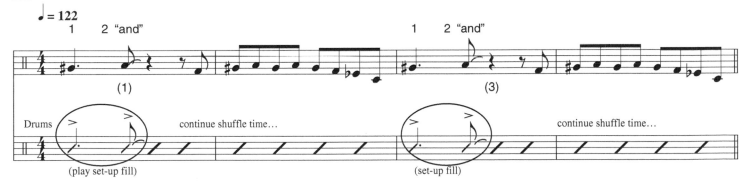

Here are some "B section" setup fills to get you started. Also try your own fills. Experiment and stay musical!

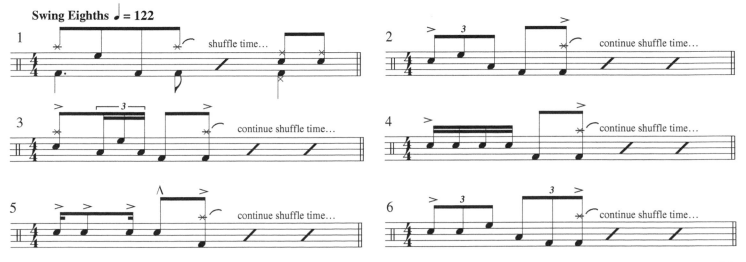

THINGS AIN'T WHAT THEY USED TO BE

—MERCER ELLINGTON

TRACK 4 with drumset   TRACK 5 without drumset

6 TWO-FEEL VS. FOUR-FEEL

Definitions

Two-Feel: Refers to the alternating emphasis of the first and third beats of the 4/4 measure, generally by the rhythm section, resulting in a half-note pulse.

Four-Feel: Refers to the emphasis of all four beats in a 4/4 measure, generally accentuated by a walking bass pattern and jazz ride cymbal pattern, resulting in a quarter-note pulse.

Typically, when the bass player plays half notes on beats 1 and 3 of a 4/4 measure, the feeling of "two" or a "two-feel" is identified. The feeling of "four" or a "four-feel" is referred to when the bass player plays four quarter notes in each measure, or "walking bass." The rest of the rhythm section plays accordingly.

Application

When playing a four-feel, the jazz ride cymbal pattern is played in the usual way. When playing a two-feel, a "broken" ride pattern can help accentuate the half-note pulse. Try the following examples:

Ride Two-Feel

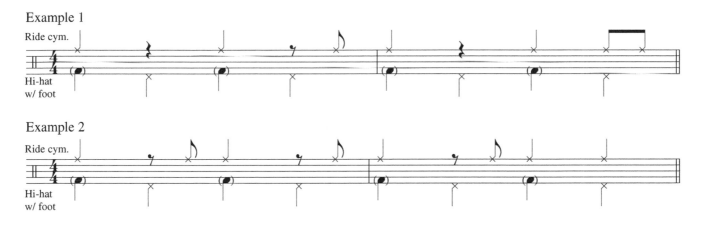

Note: It is not uncommon to play the standard jazz ride pattern when playing a two-feel. Experiment!

For more information on two-feel ride cymbal patterns, *Creative Timekeeping for the Contemporary Jazz Drummer,* by Rick Mattingly, is recommended.

Hi-Hat Two-Feel

A jazz two-feel can also be played on the hi-hat in several different ways. Try the following technique:

Open the hi-hat cymbals slightly by releasing your foot approximately one quarter of an inch (your foot should not leave the pedal). The cymbals should sizzle when struck with a stick tip. Then, softly close the cymbals by pressing down on the hi-hat pedal with your foot. (Do not close them too hard, but rather apply a small amount of pressure to the foot pedal when closing.)

The Jazz Time Pattern

When playing the jazz time pattern on the hi-hat cymbals, beats 1 and 3 should have a sizzle sound, while beats 2 and 4 should have a closed sound. Keeping your heel down with the cymbals closed, slightly raise the ball of your foot on the "and" of beats 2 and 4, opening the hi-hat cymbals 1/4 inch. To close, completely close the foot pedal on beats 2 and 4. This slight up and down motion of the foot should move in tempo and be very consistent.

JAZZ TIME HI-HAT PATTERN WITH STICK

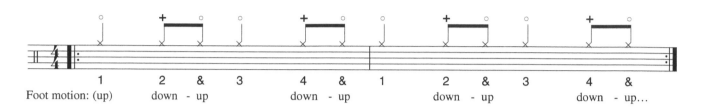

Try adding a very soft "feathered" bass drum on beats 1 and 3.

John Riley discusses another common hi-hat technique in his book *The Art of Bop Drumming*. Be sure to check it out!

Play Along: "All of Me"

Seymour Simons/Gerald Marks

Synopsis

A Few Recommended Recordings

*   Lester Young, *Jazz Memories Compilation* (recorded January 1956)

*   Sarah Vaughan, *The Essential Sarah Vaughan: The Great Songs* (recorded February 1957) Listed rhythm section: Roy Haynes, drums; Richard Davis, bass; Jimmy Jones, piano; Sarah Vaughan, vocal

*   Billie Holiday, *Billie's Blues* (recorded live in Germany, January 1954)

*   Joao Gilberto, *Amoroso/Brasil* (1977)

Tune Form and Analysis

"All of Me" has been covered by many great jazz artists, and is by far one of *the* classic standard tunes that every working jazz musician knows. The form is 32 bars made up of two 16-bar phrases. The first eight bars of each phrase are identical; however, the second eight bars of each phrase differ. Typically, the last eight bars of the tune (second phrase) would be used as an intro, immediately returning to the top for the melody and solo chorus.

Play-Along Track Arrangement

This arrangement is typical of how "All of Me" might be played on a jazz gig. The last eight bars are played as the intro with a walking "four-feel." The head is then played one time through with an accompanying "two-feel" by the rhythm section. The last two bars of the head are used to set up the "four-feel," while the soloist begins, and is continued through each solo. The saxophone plays the first solo chorus, followed by a piano solo chorus. When returning to the final head, the "two-feel" is played once again.

The "tag," which is the 29th and 30th bars of the melody, is repeated two times, setting up the "Count Basie-styled" ending.

Listen to track 6 several times while following the lead sheet. Once you're ready, give track 7 a try!

Approach

Listen carefully to track 6. The last eight bars of the tune serve as the introduction. The head is played with an underlying two-feel, while the solo choruses are played with a four-feel. Approach the two-feel with a relaxed, easy groove, playing a very soft "feathered" bass drum on beats 1 and 3. The playing of the bass drum is optional, however it provides a nice foundation to the two-feel when played correctly. Experiment with variations of the jazz ride cymbal pattern (see two-feel ride examples 1 and 2).

ALL OF ME

—SEYMOUR SIMONS/GERALD MARKS

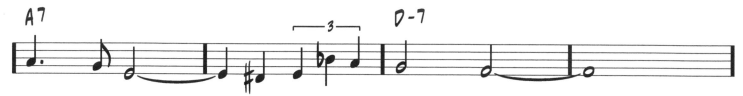

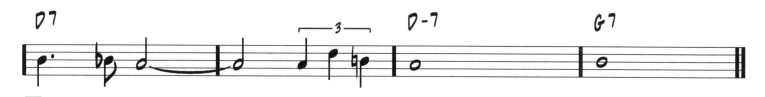

7 TRADING FOURS

Definition

The term "trading fours" is most often used to describe the alternating (or trading) of four-bar solo phrases between any solo instrumentalist and the drummer. In fact, any two solo instruments can "trade fours" during the solo section of a tune arrangement, as if they are carrying on a logical conversation or exchange of musical ideas. Alternating one-, two-, or eight-bar solo phrases are also possible.

Application

Things to Remember When Trading Fours and Soloing

- Keep the time steady when playing your solos; don't rush! Practice with a metronome at different tempos.

- Allow your solo phrases to be motivated by a specific rhythm or musical idea.

- Listen and respond to what the other soloists are playing and presenting. Play something that reflects what you hear.

- Don't overplay. Instead, play as though you are speaking. Take breaths, leave space, develop phrases and ideas with variations. Be conversational!

There are many great recordings of "trading fours," or drum soloing within a tune. Listening to the masters, such as Max Roach on Sonny Rollins's *Saxophone Colossus,* or Philly Joe Jones on *Workin' with the Miles Davis Quintet,* is vital to the development of this concept. Other great drummers to check out are Elvin Jones, Kenny Clarke, and Roy Haynes, among others. See the Resource section of this book for a listing of jazz recordings.

TRACK 8
Trading Fours
Practice Track

Triplet Exercises

Listen to track 8, ♩ = 188, the trading fours practice track (32 bars). You will hear four bars of a piano solo, then four measures of click. Play the jazz time feel during the piano solo (the first four bars of the following exercise), then play the drum solo (last four bars) during the four measures of click. Repeat each exercise four times (one time through track 8). The triplets should get you moving around the drumset and spark some melodic ideas for development. If needed, use a metronome and start with slower tempos, working up to the recorded practice track.

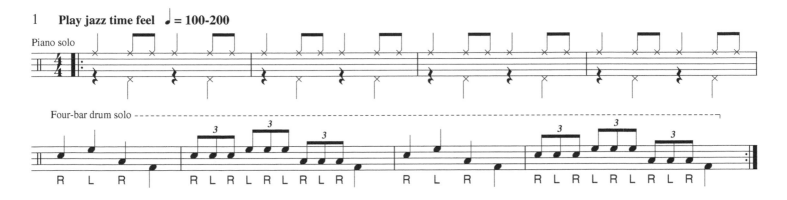

2 **Play jazz time feel (swing eighths)**

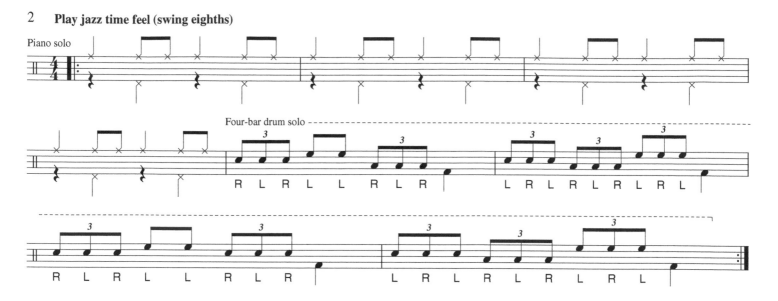

Practice playing eighth-note triplets around the drumset using both of the sticking patterns indicated.

Experiment with your own alternative sticking patterns. Use track 8, looped, or a metronome.

3

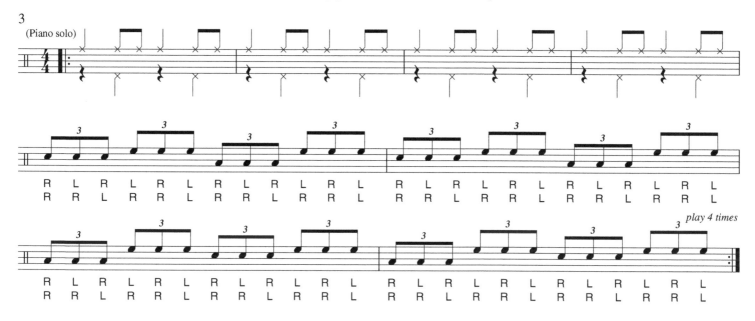

In this exercise, the bass drum becomes an extension of the hands:

4

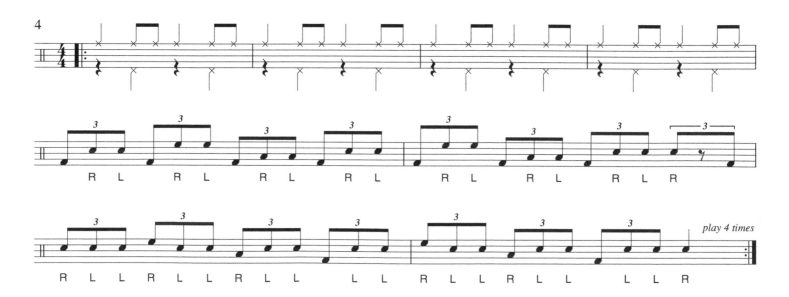

The following exercises will help you transition from triplet eighths to even eighth and sixteenth notes. The "2" indicates "even" eighth notes over a triplet (swung) pulse or subdivision, implying a two-against-three (2:3) *polyrhythm*. The sixteenth notes are played in the same way, implying a four-against-three (4:3) polyrhythm. Be sure to divide the beats evenly and keep the time steady. Remember, only the eighth notes with a "2" over them should be played evenly; all others should be played as swing (triplet) eighths. As before, use track 8 or a metronome.

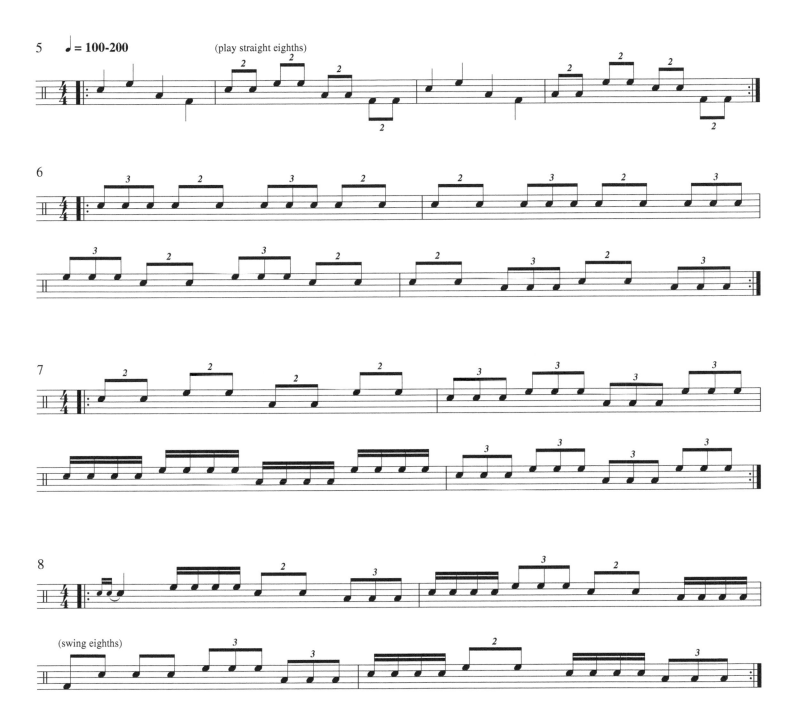

Solo Phrase Development

The following study demonstrates how to orchestrate a solo phrase or idea around the drumset. Phrases 1 through 3 use the "call and response" concept: The first and third measures represent the "call" or idea, while the second and fourth measures are the "response." Phrase 4 is a two-bar "theme" with a two-bar "variation."

Using track 8, play four measures of jazz time under the first piano solo, then play drum solo 1 (first ending). At the end of solo 1, repeat back to the top and play four more bars of jazz time under the second piano solo, then play solo 2 (second ending), and so on. Track 8 will stop after solo 4. Play groups 2 and 3 in the same way. Be sure to loop track 8 for continuous practice. For more information on trading fours and solo development, check out John Riley's book, *The Art of Bop Drumming,* or John Ramsay's *The Drummer's Complete Vocabulary, as taught by Alan Dawson.*

In the next set of solo phrases below, all of the eighth notes are swung unless otherwise indicated with a "2." Review previous exercises 5–8 in this lesson, if needed.

A "stick shot" is a stick-on-stick accent. The left stick, with tip firmly touching the snare head, is struck by the right stick. Jazz greats such as Buddy Rich and Louie Bellson used this technique quite often when soloing. Practice with track 8!

To hear an example of these solo phrases, listen to track 7 at 1:59. ♩ = 200 BPM.

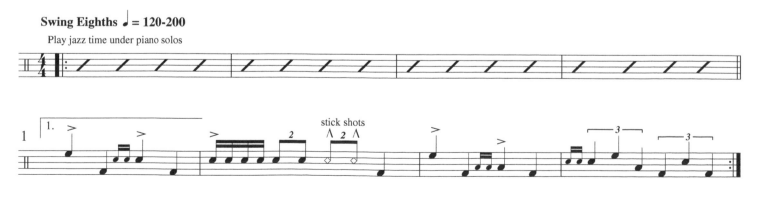

Polyrhythmic ideas can also be developed by playing a continuous figure "over the barline." This type of rhythm implies "metric modulation," in which the rhythmic figure becomes the new pulse or quarter note. If needed, play quarter notes with the bass drum, but remove them once you are comfortable with the figure (the quarter-note beat slashes will help you relate the polyrhythm to each downbeat). It is important to count aloud while learning the following rhythms! Practice with track 8!

Practice "filling in" around the polyrhythmic figure to add interest. Experiment with your own phrases and variations.

Additional variation of #2

Play-Along: "Take the 'A' Train"

Billy Strayhorn

Synopsis

A Few Recommended Recordings

- Duke Ellington and his Orchestra, *Ellington Uptown* (recorded 1953). Personnel: Ellington Orchestra; Duke and Billy Strayhorn, piano; Wendell Marshall, bass; Louie Bellson, drums; Betty Roche, vocal

- Duke Ellington, *16 Most Requested Songs* (recorded June 30, 1960). Personnel: Ellington Orchestra, Duke Ellington, piano; Sam Woodyard, drums; Aaron Bell, bass

- Dexter Gordon, *Jazz Masters Series Volume 3*

Tune Form and Analysis

This melody is a 32-bar, AABA form, and is considered one of Billy Strayhorn's most important contributions to the Ellington Orchestra. The opening piano motif is immediately recognizable and brings to mind celebrated moments of the big band era. Many versions of the tune have remained popular over the years. Even Ellington re-invented it by creating new arrangements on several different occasions. If you have the opportunity to listen to the *Ellington Uptown* version, you will hear a great re-arrangement that weaves in and out of piano figures and tempos—much different than Duke's well-remembered original, recorded in 1941. Louie Bellson's brush work is flawless on the *Uptown* recording.

Play-Along Track Arrangement

This is a typical 32-bar arrangement with an eight-bar Ellington-styled piano intro. The head (melody) is played one time through with a stop on the second-to-last measure. This stop sets up the solo piano chorus, followed by one complete chorus of trading fours with the *alternate* melody (see example). The head is played one more complete time, straight into the ending figure. Have fun!

Approach

As you listen to track 9, notice that this arrangement is played with a constant four feel. The piano intro is twice as long as Ellington's four-bar original version, but the same as Dexter Gordon's version. The jazz hi-hat pattern (example below) should be played throughout the intro, as well as the "trading fours" section. During the A sections of the head, play the jazz ride cymbal pattern, while outlining the melody with the bass drum and snare drum. Also, try "setting-up" various spots of the melody with simple drum fills. A cross-stick on beat 4 works well in each measure of the B section. Comp through the piano solo.

Play the following jazz hi-hat pattern through the piano intro:

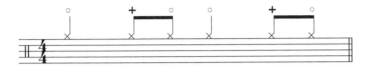

Trading Fours Applied

After the piano solo chorus, the band plays an alternate four-bar melody line (or shout chorus) during bars 1–4 of section A. The drums answer with a four-bar solo. The A section then repeats and is played in the same way, bars 9–12, followed by another four-bar drum solo (see example below). The bass then solos through B, returning back to A, which is played as before.

Form (trading fours section): AABA; (A) alt melody/drums; (A) alt melody/drums; (B) bass solo; (A) alt melody/drums.

TAKE THE "A" TRAIN

TRACK 9
with drumset

TRACK 10
without drumset

-BILLY STRAYHORN

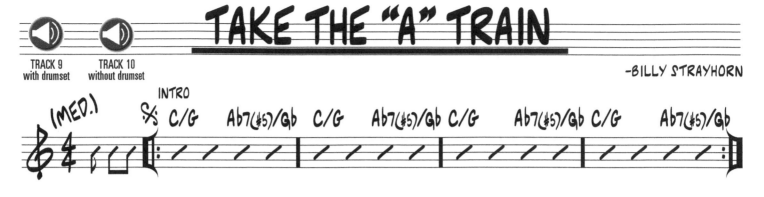

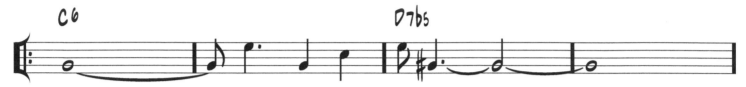

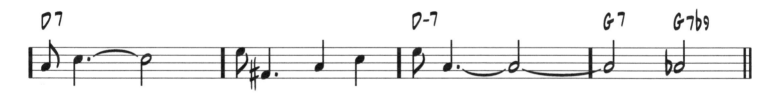

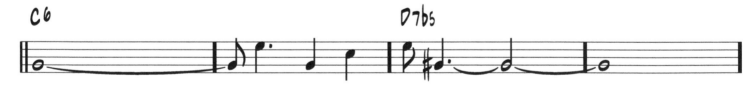

AFTER SOLOS, D.S. AL ⊕

8 BRUSHES

Background

Developing good brush technique is essential when playing jazz styles. Furthermore, brush textures and sounds are very versatile, which means they can be used in other genres of music as well. Every drummer should own a pair of wire brushes and know the sounds they make. Different models are available by several manufacturers. Experiment with a brush that feels good and suits your playing needs.

There are many excellent drumset books dealing with the art of playing brushes. For the purpose of this book, however, we will cover only a few basic patterns and exercises. For more in-depth information on brush technique and development, the following books are highly recommended:

* *Drumset Essentials: Volumes 2 and 3,* by Peter Erskine
* *The Sound of Brushes,* by Ed Thigpen
* *The Art of Bop Drumming,* by John Riley
* *Brushworks,* by Clayton Cameron

Also, take time to listen to jazz "brushmasters," such as Ed Thigpen, Clayton Cameron, and Jeff Hamilton, to name a few. Check out as many great recordings as possible (see the Resource section at the end of this book).

Hand Position

If you are unfamiliar with brush techniques, the following examples and exercises will get you started. When playing the brushes, the hands move both vertically and horizontally. The traditional grip is preferred (see the following photos), but not required. If you are uncomfortable with the traditional grip, stay with the matched grip (see brush photos 1–5).

There are three primary brush strokes: sweep, shade, and tap.

THE SWEEP

Lift your hands waist high, turning your palms so they face each other with thumbs on top, as if you are shaking someone's hand. Now, move your hands side-to-side in a fluid motion, simulating a snake in the water, or a fish's tail, keeping the wrists and fingers flexible. The sweep is a horizontal motion, which requires this type of side-to-side hand movement (see photos 6–8).

Now, try this same hand motion with your brushes on the snare drum. Making large circles, left hand clockwise, right hand counterclockwise, move the tips of the wire brushes smoothly around the snare drum. Do not press down too hard, but rather let them stir lightly on the top of the drumhead. (Note: Extending the right index finger down the shaft of the brush may be helpful. When playing matched grip, extend both the left and right index fingers: See brush photos 9–12.)

Brush Photo Examples

1. Traditional grip: tap position

2. Matched grip: tap position

3. Traditional grip: sweep position

4. Matched grip: sweep position

5. Traditional grip:
sweep position–left hand

When sweeping, the left hand should be positioned slightly over the top of the brush handle, as in photo 5.

Hand Positions: The Sweep

Photo 6   Photo 7   Photo 8

With Brushes: The Sweep

Photo 9   Photo 10

Left Hand: Clockwise Sweep

Photo 11   Photo 12

Right Hand: Counterclockwise Sweep

Practice making smooth, legato circles several times, with each hand (as illustrated), until you are comfortable with this motion. Move the circles in tempo, playing the hi-hat on beats 2 and 4 with your foot. Keep the sound of the brush constant and unchanging. Practice with a metronome to keep a steady pulse.

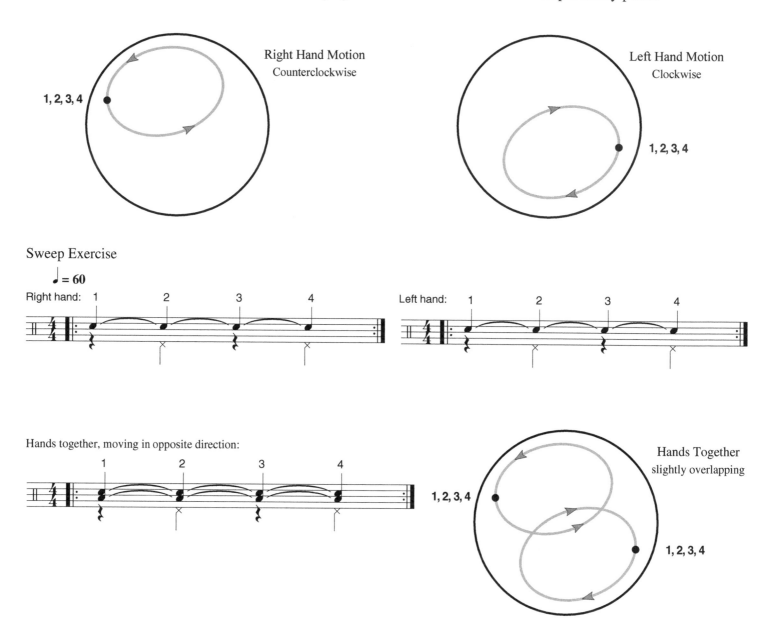

Shading

Play the brushes in the same way as the sweep, with the tips circling lightly around the snare head. While continuing this motion, simply apply pressure into the drumhead, using the wire to create a louder sweeping sound (see photos 13 & 14). This is called "shading." Shading is used to *accent* various parts of a rhythmic brush pattern using short, quick strokes, or long, smooth strokes. Experiment with the many sweeping and shading sounds you can create with your brushes!

Jazz Ride Pattern Using the Sweep

The following example explains how to play the jazz ride pattern horizontally! Start with the right hand and use the same sweeping motion as before. Moving in circles, accent (shade) the quarter-note pulse with a quick, sideways flick of the wrist on each beat, simulating quarter notes on a ride cymbal. Extending the right index finger will help maintain a smooth sound. Remember, this is a *horizontal* motion; keep the brush on the drum at all times!

Right hand

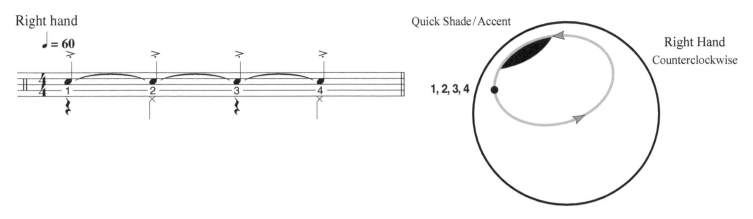

The left hand also uses the sweep motion. However, only accent (shade) the "and" or upbeat of beats 2 and 4, not the quarter-note pulse. While moving the tip of the brush in a clockwise motion, create the "upbeat" accent by applying pressure for a louder sweep. In this case, the left-hand shading strokes are longer than the right-hand strokes.

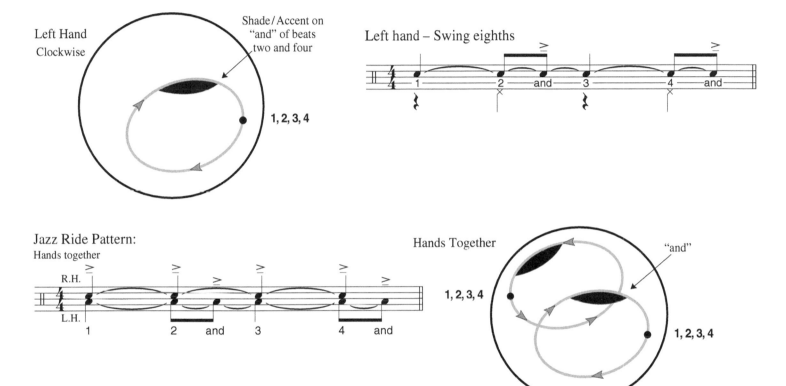

Jazz Ride Pattern:
Hands together

Shading Photo Examples

13. Right Hand Shading
"Dig in" brush wires

14. Left Hand Shading

"Digging in" with brushes creates an accented sweeping sound.

The Tap

The tap is a vertical striking motion, similar to that of the stroke made with a stick. However, since the brush doesn't rebound in the same way as a drumstick, try using a full stroke. The full stroke consists of a down and quick wrist up motion. This motion whips the tips of the brushes onto the snare head for a clean, full sound (see photos 15 & 16). Brushes make so many beautiful tones around the drumset. Experiment with them to see what musical sounds you can create!

Practice playing rudiments and warm-up exercises with your brushes. This is excellent for wrist strengthening and soloing ideas. You will definitely feel the benefits when you pick up your sticks!

The following exercises utilize various tap strokes that might be used in performance. Play each exercise several times, first leading with the right hand, then the left. Play the hi-hat on beats 2 and 4 with the foot. Start slow and work up to faster tempos.

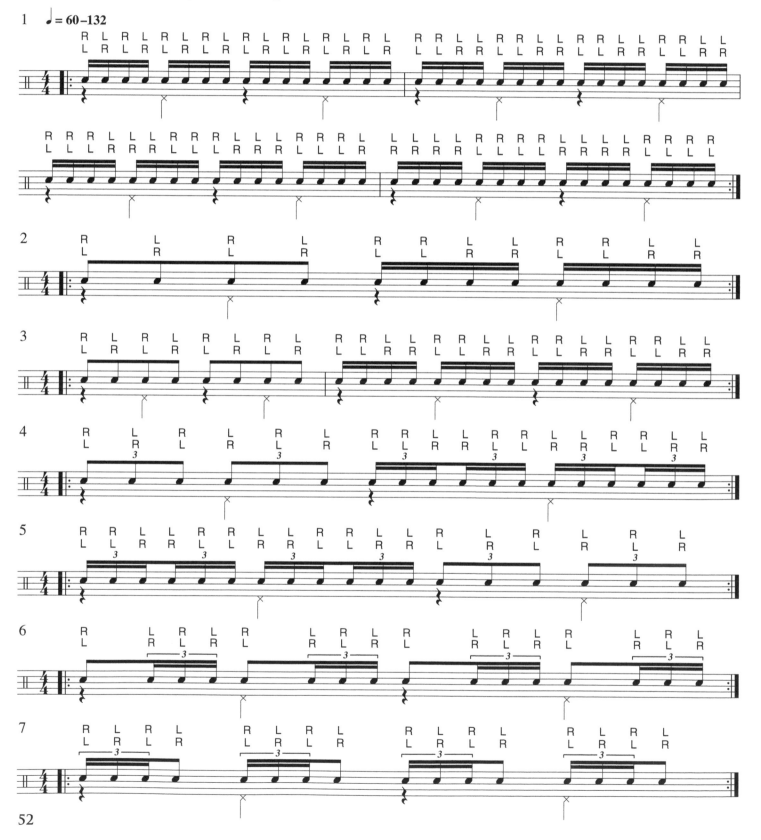

15. Right hand: downstroke

15a. Right hand: upstroke

16. Left hand: downstroke

16a. Left hand: upstroke

Additional Patterns

Here are a few basic brush patterns and illustrations to get you started. Remember to let the tips of the brushes float smoothly over the snare head, moving the circles in time! Slightly push the brush into the head when shading. The following patterns use clockwise circles in the left hand, and counterclockwise circles in the right hand. Alternately, the left hand can move counterclockwise, while the right hand moves clockwise. Experiment to see which feels best to you.

Sweeping Jazz Ride Pattern:

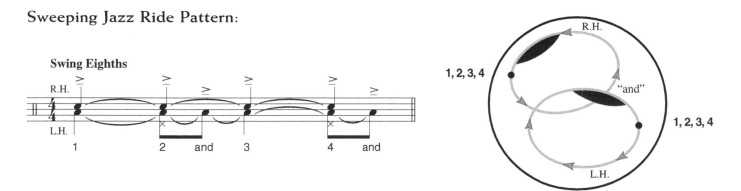

Use this one for the head of "Don't Get Around Much Anymore" track.

Medium Swing Eighths:

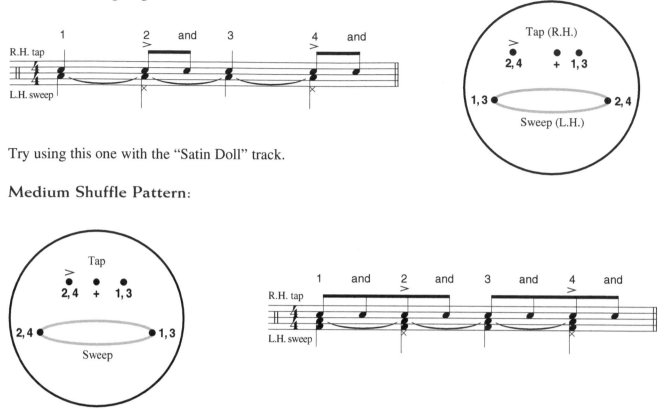

Try using this one with the "Satin Doll" track.

Medium Shuffle Pattern:

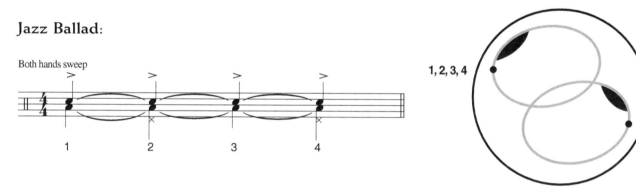

Softly play the bass drum on all four beats to the measure and maintain a balance of sound around the kit. Try this one on the B section of "Don't Get Around Much Anymore."

Jazz Ballad:

Slow Straight Eighths Jazz Ballad (subdivide 8ths):

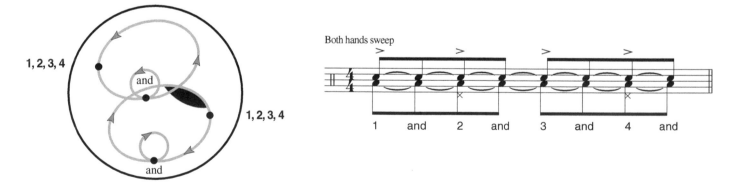

At times, the ballad tempo is so slow that it becomes difficult to play large brush circles and maintain the proper feel. Subdividing with small circles within the pattern often helps to keep the slow tempos steady. Experiment with what works well for you.

Use this pattern for "Body and Soul," track 16.

These are by no means the only brush patterns available. To learn more about the art of playing brushes, seek out private instruction, or check out the excellent books mentioned earlier in this chapter. Have fun and stay musical!

Play-Along: "Satin Doll"

Duke Ellington

Synopsis

A Few Recommended Recordings

- Duke Ellington, *16 Most Requested Songs* (recorded February 19, 1959). Personnel: Ellington Orchestra; Duke Ellington, piano; Sam Woodyard, drums; Jimmy Woode, bass
- *Lush Life: The Billy Strayhorn Songbook* (compiled 1996). Billy Eckstine: The Modern Sound of Mr. B
- *Ben Webster Meets Bill Coleman* (recorded April 27, 1967)

Tune Form and Analysis

The form is AABA. The first two A sections are identical, releasing to the bridge, or B section. The final A is exactly like the first.

This tune is simple, with a catchy, easy-to-remember melody, which is likely why it's so popular. However, it is interesting to note that Ellington collaborated on "Satin Doll" during a time when he was composing long suites, film scores, and adaptations of classical pieces for his band.

Play-Along Track Arrangement

This arrangement is simple: two full choruses, two tags, and an ending. The tune begins with the melody, without an intro (often referred to as "starting right on it"). The first chorus is the head/melody. The second chorus is part piano solo AAB, and part melody, final A. The two tags consist of the last four bars of the melody, repeated, with a recognizable standard ending. The piano and bass play alternate chord changes in the 31st and 32nd measure to set up the repeat choruses and tags.

Approach

Have fun with this classic tune! Play a basic, medium swing brush pattern, and listen closely to the melody. There are plenty of opportunities to play setup fills and to "outline the melody." Remember, this is a jazz trio setting… don't overplay! Before you begin playing track 12, listen to example track 11 several times. Keep the brushes fluid and light, and stay musical!

In this medium swing brush pattern, the right hand taps the jazz ride pattern, while the left hand sweeps the quarter-note pulse.

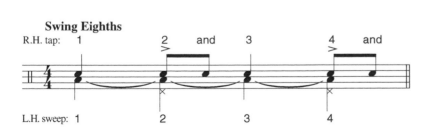

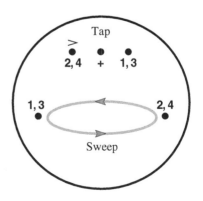

Satin Doll

TRACK 11
with drumset

TRACK 12
without drumset

–Duke Ellington

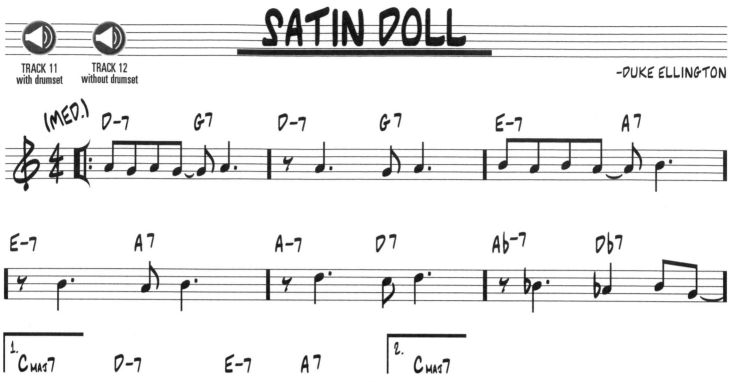

FINE

Play-Along: "Don't Get Around Much Anymore"

Duke Ellington; lyrics by Bob Russell

Synopsis

A Few Recommended Recordings

- Duke Ellington, *16 Most Requested Songs* (recorded November 20, 1947)
  Personnel: Ellington Orchestra; Duke Ellington, piano; Sonny Greer, drums; Oscar Pettiford, bass

- Nat King Cole: *Just One of Those Things* (and more)
  Nat King Cole with the Count Basie Orchestra (recorded 1958)

- Tony Bennett: *Bennett Sings Ellington Hot and Cool* (1999)
  Featured personnel: Clayton Cameron, drums; Ralph Sharon, piano; Gary Sargent, guitar; Wynton Marsalis, trumpet; with full orchestration

- Natalie Cole: *Unforgettable: With Love, Natalie Cole* (1991)
  Rhythm section: Brad Cole, piano; Harold Jones, drums; James Hughart, bass; Alfred Viola, guitar

Tune Form and Analysis

This is a wonderful composition with great lyrics! The song form is AABA, 32 bars, and is a type of antiphonal or "call and response" piece, which means separate groups of performers alternate or respond to each other. This melody follows those guidelines. There are several arrangements of this tune that utilize the "call and response" concept to a large degree, and some with a more subdued approach. Nonetheless, when a singer or instrumentalist plays a melodic line and an alternating response is heard, it qualifies.

There are so many great recordings of this tune, such as Natalie Cole's version with Harold Jones on drums. After the orchestra plays the intro, the music breaks while she sings the opening line. As she sings each melody line of the A section, the horns play a response. Ellington's 1947 version with singer Al Hibbler is similar, although slower in tempo. Tony Bennett's version is very slow and bluesy, with full orchestration.

Play-Along Track Arrangement

This jazz quartet arrangement consists of four times through the 32-bar, AABA song form. It starts "right on it," with the saxophone playing the first phrase of the melody, or the "call." The head is played one time through, followed by two solo choruses; first the piano, then the saxophone. The head plays one more time through (AABA), tags once, and ends.

Approach

In a typical small group arrangement of this standard, the horn player or vocalist plays/sings the "call," while the "response" is played by the rhythm section. This provides the drummer an opportunity to "outline the melody" and to play setup fills around the rhythmic figure, which starts on the "and" of beat 1 (example 1). The same rhythmic figure is also played in measure 1 of the first ending, setting up the second call-and-response A section. Play the sweeping jazz ride pattern with the brushes (example 2) in bars 5, 6, and 7 of the A section, each time. Continue to play time in the second ending, building dynamically into the bridge. In this section, try "digging in" by playing the medium shuffle pattern (example 3). This gives the bridge a grooving, forward motion. After the bridge, the final A section returns once again with the "call and response." In the last measure of the head, quickly put down the brushes and play the subsequent solo choruses with sticks. This provides for a nice dynamic contrast. After the saxophone solo, quickly return to the brushes to play the final head/melody chorus. The ending is typical of how it may be played on a jazz gig.

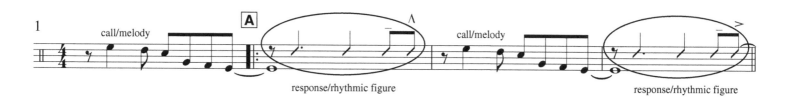

2   Sweeping Jazz Ride Pattern   3   Medium Shuffle Pattern

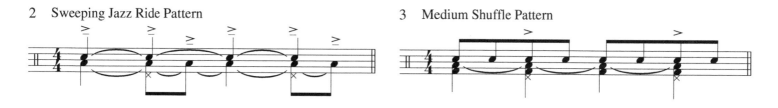

Don't Get Around Much Anymore

-Duke Ellington/Bob Russell

TRACK 13 with drumset   TRACK 14 without drumset

Play-Along: "Body and Soul"

John Green, Robert Sour, Edward Heyman, Frank Eyton

Synopsis

A Few Recommended Recordings

- Al Cohn and Zoot Sims, *Body and Soul* (recorded March 23, 1973)
  Personnel: Sims and Cohn, saxophones; Jaki Byard, piano; Mel Lewis, drums; George Duvivier, bass

- John Coltrane, *The Heavyweight Champion: The Complete Atlantic Recordings.*
  Personnel: Coltrane, tenor sax; Elvin Jones, drums; McCoy Tyner, piano; Steve Davis, bass

- Billie Holiday, *Lady in Autumn; The Best of the Verve Years* (recorded April 22, 1946)

- Bud Powell, *The Complete Bud Powell* (recorded February 1950)
  Personnel: Max Roach, drums; Curly Russell, bass; Bud Powell, piano

Tune Form and Analysis

The song form is AABA, 32 bars, and is generally played as a ballad. However, Coltrane's version is performed as a medium swing, with a reoccurring chordal piano theme that starts in the intro. On the ballad version by Al Cohn and Zoot Sims, Mel Lewis's brush and cymbal work is very fluid and understated. In the solo section, Mel orchestrates tasteful interplay around the kit using eighth-note subdivisions between the snare and hi-hat. Also, check out Billie Holiday's version on *Lady in Autumn: The Best of the Verve Years.*

Play-Along Track Arrangement

This track is fashioned after the Al Cohn, Zoot Sims version, without the solo section. The piano intro (not on the chart) is two bars in length, followed by one complete time through the head/melody (32 bars). Tag the last two bars of the head twice, ritarding to the final chord.

Approach

Maintain an even, fluid motion with the brush tips, embellishing musically in spots. Creative use of cymbal and hi-hat textures add beautiful color to ballads, such as this one. Try playing brush example 2, below. Subdividing the pattern often helps maintain a steady, straight-eighth-note pulse. The large circles in example 1 will also work, but might be difficult to keep steady at slower tempos. Use shading techniques (discussed earlier) for added interest, and feather the bass drum lightly. Experiment with patterns and sounds that you feel comfortable with, but be sure they accurately reflect the subdivision of the tune you are playing. Some ballads, such as "Misty," may be played with a triplet subdivision.

Reminder: Coated snare drum heads, or equivalent, are recommended when playing brushes.

1 Ballad brushes   2 Eighth note subdivision

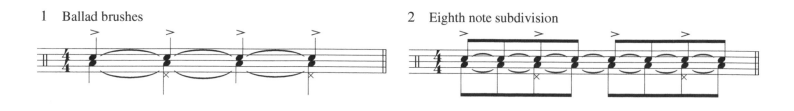

BODY AND SOUL

–John Green/Edward Heyman/
Robert Sour/Frank Eyton

TRACK 15
with drumset

TRACK 16
without drumset

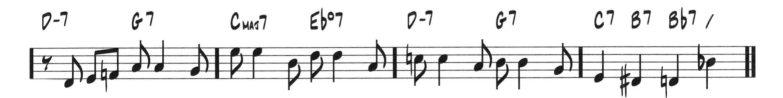

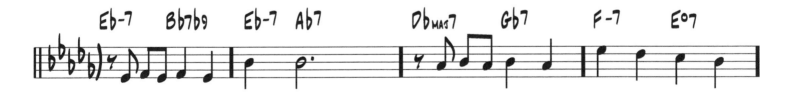

9 BEBOP

Background

World War II played an important role in the development of bebop in the 1940s. Many veteran swing-era musicians were being drafted, which provided opportunities to young, undrafted musicians anxious to move into the ranks of the touring road bands. Dizzy Gillespie, Charlie Parker, and Stan Getz were among these young musicians who developed their craft by working closely with swing masters such as Jack Teagarden and Earl Hines.

It wasn't long before war restrictions initiated the demise of the big bands. A government-imposed entertainment tax forced cut backs in dance halls. Clubs were closing, which meant the large dance bands were losing money and were unable to work.

Jazz quartets, quintets, and trios quickly emerged. As a result, many after hours clubs, such as Minton's Playhouse in Harlem, became a breeding ground for small group explorations. Along with Gillespie, Parker, and Getz, guitarist Charlie Christian, bassist Jimmy Blanton, and pianist Thelonious Monk expanded the improvisational elements by exploring more advanced harmonies, chord alterations, and substitutions.

Rhythmically, drummers began to play more freely. The regimented quarter-note pulse of the swing era bass drum shifted to the ride cymbal and bass player, while tempos got much faster. This new freedom allowed drummers like Max Roach and Kenny Clarke to interact with the soloist by creating rhythmic accents on the snare and bass drum. This is often referred to as comping.

Play-Along: "Four"

Miles Davis

Synopsis

A Few Recommended Recordings

* Miles Davis, *Workin' with The Miles Davis Quintet* (recorded May 11, 1956)
  Personnel: Miles Davis, trumpet; John Coltrane, tenor saxophone; Red Garland, piano; Paul Chambers, bass; Philly Joe Jones, drums

* *Miles Davis, The Complete Concert 1964*: *My Funny Valentine and Four and More Recorded Live in Concert.*
  Personnel: Miles Davis, trumpet; George Coleman, saxophone; Ron Carter, bass; Herbie Hancock, piano; Tony Williams, drums

* Chet Baker, *Chet Baker in Tokyo* (recorded live on June 14, 1987)

Tune Form and Analysis

The form of this tune is 32-bar ABAB' ("B'," or "B prime," meaning it differs slightly from the first B section).

"Four" was released on the LP *Workin' with The Miles Davis Quintet,* which was part of the 1956 Prestige recording sessions with the first of Davis's legendary quintets, featuring Philly Joe Jones on drums, producing 24 tracks. The music from these recording sessions was released on four albums: *Cookin', Relaxin', Workin',* and *Steamin'.* Philly Joe's drumming on this recording of "Four" is exceptional. He outlines the melody in each A section, while highlighting it throughout letter B. During his trading-fours chorus, Jones tastefully displays his musicianship and soloing abilities. His influence is timeless and definitive.

Another version of "Four" can be heard on Miles Davis's *The Complete Concert 1964: My Funny Valentine and Four and More Recorded Live in Concert.* Tony Williams's drumming performance and mastery of the ride cymbal is incredible!

Play-Along Track Arrangement

Listen to track 17. This arrangement starts at the beginning of the chart and follows the head (ABAB) one time. The saxophone then plays two solo choruses, followed by one chorus of trading fours. The head/melody is then played one complete time, ending in the 30th measure (as written). The ABAB form is played five times.

Approach

Outlining the melody is essential when playing this tune. Below, see a sample of the melody, starting at letter A. Example 1 shows how a drummer might mimic or reflect the melody on the drums. This is similar to what Philly Joe played on the *Workin' with The Miles Davis Quintet* version.

Use of the snare and cymbals reflects the motion of the melody, but not necessarily the long and short tones. Experiment with different tone qualities by playing example 1 around the drumset. Stay musical and don't overshadow the melody!

Play time in the B section, setting up and accenting the high points in the third and seventh measures (example 2).

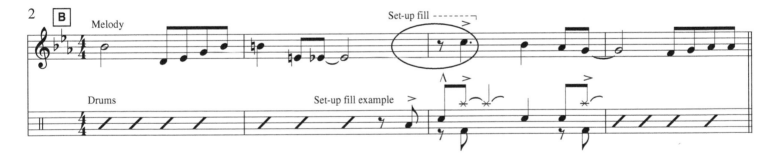

In the second ending, accent the melodic figures (see example 3). Highlighting and accenting various parts of the melody is common practice when playing bebop. The melodic figures are circled below.

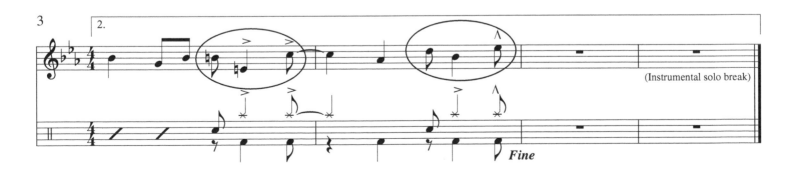

Four

TRACK 17
with drumset

TRACK 18
without drumset

—MILES DAVIS

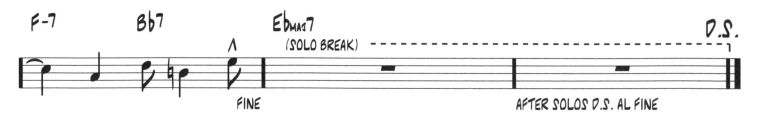

FINE

AFTER SOLOS D.S. AL FINE

JAZZ WALTZ

Background

The waltz is a dance that originated in the suburbs of Vienna and became popular in Viennese dance halls in late eighteenth century. More than any other dance, the waltz appeared to represent the new era paradigms of passion, freedom, and expressiveness as it erupted into international popularity by the late 1700s.

The term waltz comes from the German word "waltzen," which means "to turn or rotate." This dance is done in 3/4 time, with an accent on the first beat of every measure. Musically, the waltz is very refined and orchestrated. Instrumentation for these pieces often included the piano, violin, and the bass. Notable composers who frequently wrote in waltz time were Mozart and Johann Strauss.

Throughout the evolution of jazz, the influence of European musical styles is apparent. Such is the case with the jazz waltz. Jazz musicians utilized traditional waltz-type melodies, which were easily played over an underlying swing pulse. Equally, the more refined waltz (dance) became popular during the dance band era.

Not unlike the traditional waltz, the rhythmic emphasis of the Jazz Waltz is generally on the first beat of each measure, with less emphasis on beats two and three (boom chick-chick). This is often referred to as the feeling of "one."

Popular Jazz Waltz melodies include: "Waltz for Debby," "My Favorite Things," "Someday My Prince Will Come," and "Bluesette," among others.

Play-Along: "Bluesette"

Jean Thielemans

Synopsis

A Few Recommended Recordings

- Toots Thielemans, *The Brasil Project* (1992). Personnel: Oscar Castro-Neves, rhythm guitar; Brian Bromberg, bass; Paulinho Da Costa, percussion; Lee Ritenour, acoustic guitar

- *Buddy Rich/Mel Tormé: Together Again for the First Time* (recorded 1978).
  Personnel: The Buddy Rich Big Band; Buddy Rich, drums; Mel Tormé, vocals

- Hank Jones, *Live at Maybeck Recital Hall, Volume 16* (1992). Personnel: Hank Jones, solo piano

Tune Form and Analysis

This is a beautiful jazz waltz written by Belgian harmonica soloist Toots Thielemans, with lyrics written by Norman Gimbel. The form consists of three eight-bar phrases—A, B, C—which make up the 24-bar melody. The first two bars of the final phrase resemble the first two measures of the tune, up one-half step. It then departs from this for the final cadence. The B section, or bridge, clearly departs from, and separates, the first and third phrases. Typically, this tune is performed at a medium jazz waltz tempo.

Play-Along Track Arrangement

Listen closely to track 19. The arrangement is as follows: Eight bars intro (not on the chart), followed by one time through the head/melody (ABC), two choruses of piano solo, two choruses of saxophone solo, and a return to the head one final time. Tag the last four bars once, and end with the eight-bar outro (same as the intro).

Approach

The head is played with the feeling of "one," indicating the bass player will generally strike one sustained note on the downbeat of each measure. However, the solo sections are played in "three." In this case, the bass player plays three quarter notes to the bar, or a walking bass line. This ("one-feel" vs. a "three-feel") corresponds to a "two-feel" and "four-feel" when playing in 4/4 time.

The intro should be played lightly on the cymbals in "one." When playing the head, establish the jazz waltz with the bass drum and hi-hat (see example A). Throughout the solo section, comp musically in support of each soloist. When playing in "three," the ride cymbal and hi-hat become the focus of the time feel, while the snare drum and bass drum comp lightly.

Basic Jazz Waltz Examples

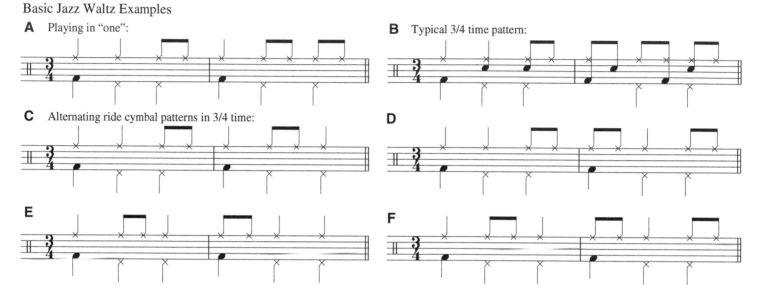

Try playing the hi-hat on beat 2 only, or beat 3 of each measure:

Use the 3/4-time pattern below to accompany the following bass drum/snare drum comping phrases. Use the above ride patterns C–H, or experiment with your own jazz waltz ride patterns and comping phrases. Try converting some of the 4/4 comping exercises from lesson 2. This should get you started!

3/4 Time Pattern

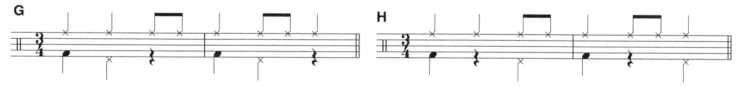

66

Bluesette

—Jean Thielemans/Norman Gimbel

11 BOSSA NOVA/SAMBA

Bossa Nova

The bossa nova is a Brazilian dance made popular in the late 1950s and 1960s, and is derived from the Brazilian samba. The samba is traditionally made up of only percussion instruments (batucada), such as the surdo drum, tamborim, caixa, cuica, ago-go bells, panderio, and ganza, playing complex rhythms. However, in the style of the bossa nova, these percussion sounds have been translated to the drumset.

By slowing down the samba and applying sophisticated arrangements and jazz chord structures, Joao Gilberto and Antonio Carlos Jobim gave form to a new style of Brazilian music called the bossa nova, meaning "new trend." In the early 1960s, the bossa nova became known throughout the United States, influencing American jazz musicians such as Stan Getz and Charlie Byrd. In 1963, the huge success of "The Girl from Ipanema" established the bossa nova as an important part of American jazz. Many jazz standards are often written and performed in the style of the bossa nova and can be found throughout the *Real Book*.

The first thing to understand about Afro-Caribbean music is the clave rhythm. There are two basic clave patterns: the 3:2 son clave, and the reverse 2:3 son clave. The choice of which to play is based upon the phrasing of the melody. Listen to as many recordings as possible to gain a greater understanding of clave rhythms (see the Resource section).

CLAVE PATTERNS

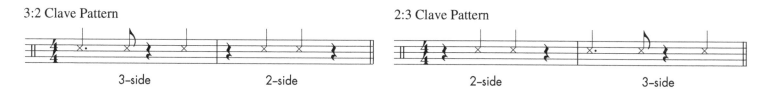

The Brazilian clave is a variation of the above clave pattern. The difference is in the "2-side" of the pattern.

For a creative variation on the bossa nova beat, use a brush on the snare drum or floor tom to emulate the guiro pattern (this works best if using coated heads). The cross-stick, bass drum, and hi-hat play as before. Play the brush sweeps as legato (long) as possible.

PARTIDO ALTO RHYTHM

The partido alto rhythm is often played by the accompanying guitar. These bossa patterns feature variations of this rhythm:

Partido Alto Rhythm

For a greater understanding of the bossa nova, the following books are recommended:

- *Brazilian Rhythms for Drumset,* by Duduka Da Fonseca and Bob Weiner
- *Practical Applications: Afro-Caribbean Rhythms for the Drum Set,* by Chuck Silverman
- *Drumset Essentials, Volume 3*, by Peter Erskine

BOSSA NOVA PATTERNS

Feel the patterns with a slow, swaying "two-feel." The bass guitar plays the same rhythmic pattern as the bass drum, which emulates the surdo drum. The hi-hat replaces the shaker, while the clave is played with a cross-stick on the snare drum.

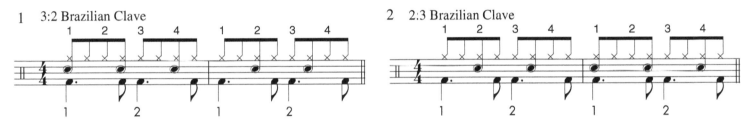

Same as above with eighth notes on the ride cymbal and hi-hat with the foot on beats 2 and 4.

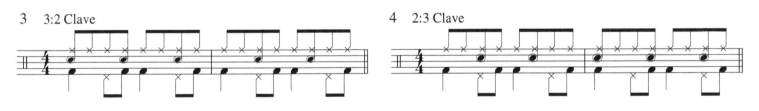

In example 5, the guiro pattern is simulated with an open/closed hi-hat:

In example 6, opening the hi-hat only on beat 3 emulates the accent of the low surdo drum:

The next few examples use a brush in the right hand on the snare, replacing the hi-hat, which now plays on beat 2 and 4 with the foot. Play the cross-stick and bass drum as before.

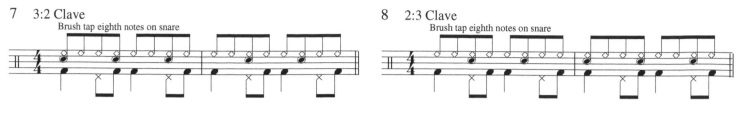

Play-Along: "The Girl from Ipanema" (Garôta De Ipanema)

Antonio Carlos Jobim/Norman Gimbel/Vinicius de Moraes

Synopsis

A Few Recommended Recordings

- Stan Getz, *Getz/Gilberto Featuring Antonio Carlos Jobim* (recorded March 1963)
  Personnel: Stan Getz, tenor sax; Antonio Carlos Jobim, piano; Joao Gilberto, guitar/ vocals; Tommy Williams, bass; Milton Banana, drums; Astrud Gilberto, vocals

- Oscar Peterson, *We Get Requests* (recorded 1965)
  Personnel: Ed Thigpen, drums; Ray Brown, bass; Oscar Peterson, piano

- Antonio Carlos Jobim, *Novabossa: Red Hot on Verve*

Tune Form and Analysis

The tune form is 40-bar, AABA, with a 16-bar bridge.

With the presence of saxophonist Stan Getz, guitarist Joao Gilberto, vocalist Astrud Gilberto, and composer/pianist Antonio Carlos Jobim, "The Girl from Ipanema" attained worldwide status in 1963. It has since become among the most recorded standards to date. In fact, this Getz/Gilberto collaboration yielded four Grammy® Awards and remained on the pop charts for 96 weeks! As a result, the bossa nova style became a significant new ingredient to American jazz. Other noteworthy bossa tunes include "Desafinado" and "Corcovado."

Play-Along Track Arrangement

Listen to track 21. This arrangement is two times through the form, with the last four measures of the lead sheet serving as the four-bar intro (intro not notated at the top of the chart).

The 40-bar, AABA melody is played one complete time. During the solo chorus, the piano plays the first 16 measures (AA), followed by the tenor saxophone over the 16-bar bridge (B). At the completion of the bridge, the melody returns in the final A section. Tag the last two bars twice for the outro, ritarding to the last note. This is a typical ending.

Approach

Play the 3:2 Brazilian clave through the intro, outro, and A sections (example 1). The use of a brush and a stick is very effective. In the bridge, try "opening up" the groove with the light cymbals and toms (example 2). There are many options when playing the bossa nova. Experiment with what feels good to you, and works for the song performance. Be sure to keep the time steady, and maintain a groove that is appropriate to the bossa style. Take time to find and listen to the bossa nova!

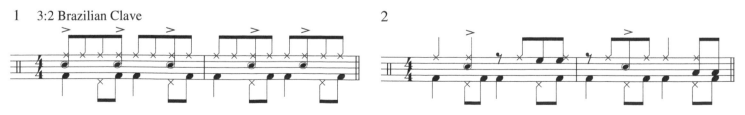

The Girl From Ipanema
(Garôta De Ipanema)

—Antonio Carlos Jobim/Norman Gimbel/Vinicius De Moraes

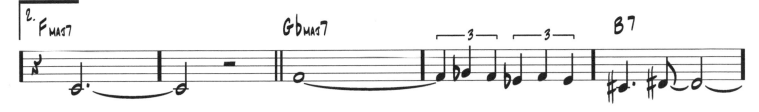

Samba

The samba is deeply rooted in Brazilian musical/dance traditions, and is often referred to as the musical lifeblood of Brazil. There are many variations of samba, due largely to the different regions of the country. However, in the early 1900s, it became most prominent among the working class of Rio de Janeiro and a major part of the street celebration during Carnival.

As the popularity of the samba grew worldwide, jazz artists of the 1950s and 1960s incorporated its style and 2/4 meter into their compositions. As a result, jazz standards are commonly played in the samba style.

The samba is played at a faster tempo than the bossa nova, and is felt with a two-feel with a slight accent on beat 2. It can either be written in 2/4 or cut-time. Either way, the feel remains the same. For the purpose of this book, the patterns will be written in 2/4 time.

The following examples 1–6 show each part of a basic jazz samba pattern, played on the drumset. The bass drum pattern again resembles the surdo drum. As in example 1, try playing a slight accent only on beat 2; however, be careful to not overplay. The feeling of the samba is light, not heavy. Example 2 shows the addition of the hi-hat, played with the foot.

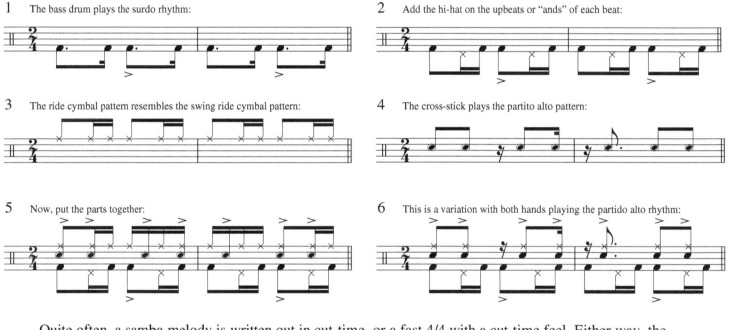

1   The bass drum plays the surdo rhythm:

2   Add the hi-hat on the upbeats or "ands" of each beat:

3   The ride cymbal pattern resembles the swing ride cymbal pattern:

4   The cross-stick plays the partito alto pattern:

5   Now, put the parts together:

6   This is a variation with both hands playing the partido alto rhythm:

Quite often, a samba melody is written out in cut-time, or a fast 4/4 with a cut-time feel. Either way, the samba pattern still sounds like sixteenth notes, even though it is written as eighth notes. Note: Example 7 sounds like example 8. For more information on reading rhythms, check out *The Encyclopedia of Reading Rhythms* by Gary Hess.

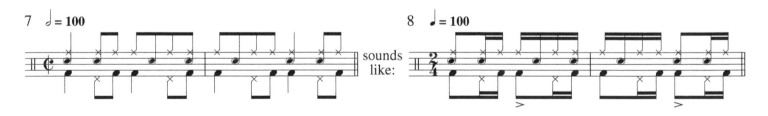

7   ♩ = 100

sounds like:

8   ♩ = 100

The samba is frequently played with brushes. Here are two examples:

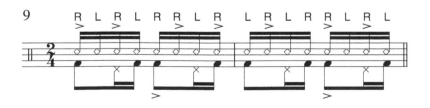

9   R L R L R R L R   L R L R R R L R L

In this example, play the brush pattern on the snare with the right hand, and the partido alto rhythm with a cross-stick in the left hand.

There are many different ways to approach the samba. To learn more about its rhythmic patterns and traditions, the following books are highly recommended:

* *Brazilian Rhythms for Drumset,* by Duduka Da Fonseca and Bob Weiner
* *Practical Applications: Afro-Caribbean Rhythms for the Drum Set*, by Chuck Silverman
* *Drumset Essentials, Volume 3*, by Peter Erskine
* *The Drummer's Bible,* by Mick Berry and Jason Gianni

Seek out and listen to as much Brazilian music as possible!

Play-Along: "St. Thomas"

Sonny Rollins

Synopsis

A Few Recommended Recordings

* Sonny Rollins, *Saxophone Colossus* (recorded June 22, 1956). Personnel: Sonny Rollins, saxophone; Tommy Flanagan, piano; Doug Watkins, bass; Max Roach, drums
* Joshua Redman, *Spirit of the Moment: Live at the Village Vanguard* (recorded March 1965; two-disc set). Personnel: Joshua Redman, saxophone; Brian Blade, drums; Peter Martin, piano; Christopher Thomas, bass

Tune Form and Analysis

The tune form is ABAB, 32 bars. The head is actually 16 bars in length (AB), but is always repeated (ABAB). Sonny Rollins's version of "St. Thomas," on his *Saxophone Colossus* recording, is the standard by which all others are compared. Equally, Max Roach's drum solo is wholly musical and thematic. Truly inspired!

Joshua Redman's version is also outstanding! Redman solos (unaccompanied) over the form for four-and-a-half minutes before the band enters, referencing the melody and quoting Rollins throughout. When the band does kick in, a bright samba ensues. Both of these recordings are brilliant performances.

Play-Along Track Arrangement

Listen to track 23. This arrangement, played as a samba, loosely resembles the *Saxophone Colossus* version without the swing section. The eight-bar snare drum intro pays tribute to Roach. The piano and bass enter for an additional eight bars of intro before the melody begins (chart begins with melody). When the 16-bar melody enters, it is played twice (ABAB), followed by three 16-bar (AB) saxophone solo choruses, and three 16-bar piano solo choruses. After the piano solo, the head/melody returns and is again played twice (ABAB). Tag the last four bars to end.

Approach

The drum intro is played on the snare drum with snares off. Example 1 shows the hand pattern. There are three sounds within the pattern: the cross-stick, rim shot, and open "snares off," or tenor drum sound. The addition of the bass drum and hi-hat, as shown in example 2, completes the pattern. This modified samba, which is similar to what Max played on the *Saxophone Colossus* version, continues up to the first solo.

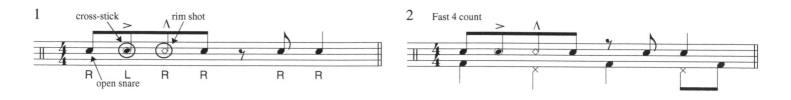

When the saxophone solo begins, play a jazz samba pattern, while ad-libbing the snare drum (example 3). Continue playing this pattern to the end of the tune. Be sure to maintain a steady tempo and stay musical!

The partido alto rhythm is used throughout this arrangement, specifically during the piano solo and last two melody choruses. Try playing the jazz samba pattern with this rhythm on the snare drum, as indicated in example 4a.

Or, try it with a cross-stick:

In this example, both hands are playing the partido alto rhythm, accompanied by the "samba feet." This helps to create rhythmic intensity.

St. Thomas

–SONNY ROLLINS

12 JAZZ ROCK/FUSION

The blending of jazz and rock styles is often referred to as "jazz rock," or "fusion." Some defining characteristics of this progressive style of music include electric keyboards and guitars, modal improvisation, funk rhythms, odd time signatures, rock textures, and sophisticated compositions and arrangements.

Throughout the 1960s, the direction of American popular music began to shift from the complexities of jazz to the music of the Beatles, Jimi Hendrix, James Brown, Sly Stone, and the politically motivated folk music of Bob Dylan. As rock and soul music became more appealing to a younger audience, jazz musicians were forced to question their conventional approaches to jazz. Innovator Miles Davis chose a new direction that integrated the rhythmic and harmonic elements of rock and soul music with contemporary jazz. This music became known as fusion.

Miles' earliest experiment with fusion is documented on his 1968 recording *Miles in the Sky*. In particular, the tune "Stuff," often referred to as the birth of this musical style, features Herbie Hancock on electric piano and Tony Williams on drums. Other notable Miles Davis recordings which helped to pave the way for this new direction in jazz are *In a Silent Way* and the commercially successful *Bitches Brew*.

In the late '60s and 1970s, many Big Band leaders such as Woody Herman, Duke Ellington, Buddy Rich and Louis Bellson were equally narrowing the generation gap by blending contemporary pop, rock, and gospel elements within their jazz arrangements, without having compromised their musical integrity. Popular songs and melodies were rearranged and re-harmonized to accommodate the more traditional jazz orchestra instrumentation.

The evolution of fusion continued in the 1970s with the emergence of several "supergroups." Among the most notable of these groups are Weather Report, led by Josef Zawinul and Wayne Shorter; Return To Forever, led by Chick Corea; The Mahavishnu Orchestra, led by John McLaughlin; and the Brecker Brothers, led by Michael and Randy Brecker. Other important fusion groups were led by Herbie Hancock, Tony Williams, and Larry Coryell.

Concurrently, rock musicians began to infuse jazz elements into their music. Groups such as The Jimi Hendrix Experience, The Grateful Dead, and Cream began to experiment with freeform improvisation, while groups such as Chicago; Blood, Sweat and Tears; and Frank Zappa's Mothers Of Invention were incorporating the more sophisticated harmonic and melodic components of jazz.

Play-Along: "Mercy, Mercy, Mercy"
Josef Zawinul

Synopsis

A Few Recommended Recordings

*   Cannonball Adderley, *The Capitol Years* (recorded October 20, 1966).
    Personnel: Cannonball Adderley, alto sax; Nat Adderley, cornet; Joe Zawinul, piano; Victor Gaskin, bass; Roy McCordy, drums

*   The Buddy Rich Band, *Mercy, Mercy* (recorded live at Caesar's Palace)

*   Herbie Mann, *Deep Pocket* (recorded 1992)

*   Howard Roberts, *Jaunty-Jolly: The Howard Roberts Quartet.* Personnel: Shelly Manne, drums; Howard Roberts, guitar; Dave Grusin, organ; Chuck Berghofer, bass

Tune Form and Analysis

The style of this tune resembles that of a gospel song or hymn: Verse and chorus, with a chorus tag or transition. The melody form is 20 bars in length—A (8 bars), B (4 bars), C (4 bars), D (4 bars)—and is generally performed in a straight-eighths jazz rock or funk style, depending on the version you listen to. Cannonball Adderley's live version (with Joe Zawinul on piano) is slow and bluesy with gospel overtones. Buddy Rich's jazz-rock version is a well-arranged Phil Wilson big band chart, quicker in tempo, weaving through modulations. There are many other arrangements that range from smooth jazz to hip-hop.

Play-Along Track Arrangement

Listen to track 25. The arrangement is four times through the 20-bar form. The first four bars of the lead sheet are played as the intro, followed by the head/melody played one complete time through. The tenor saxophone plays one solo chorus, followed by a piano solo chorus. The head returns, ritarding in the last two measures to end the arrangement.

Approach

Play letter A at a mezzo forte dynamic level, as you would the verse of a song. The B and C sections should build in dynamic intensity throughout the eight bars, and then quickly reduce for the D section.

The following are the three groove patterns performed on track 25. Playing a closed hi-hat at letter A will help maintain the medium dynamic level. In letter B, open up by increasing the dynamic intensity with the ride cymbal. The bass and snare drums should remain solid throughout the performance, yet reflect the appropriate dynamic level. Feel free to use different groove patterns. If you find that a cross-stick sound works best in the A section, then do it! Experiment and trust your instincts. However, make sure whatever you play is motivated by your performance of the tune, not the ability to impress others! Express yourself musically and have fun.

Play this pattern for the intro and A section of the head. Feel free to ad lib with "ghost strokes," but stay musical.

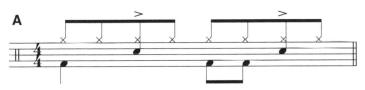

Play this pattern in the B section. Use of the ride cymbal and ride bell provide new textures to the B section, while increasing the dynamic level.

This note is not played in the first chorus, but is played in the remaining choruses.

Each time in the final C section, the bass drum should accent this rhythm with the rest of the band.

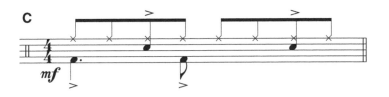

MERCY, MERCY, MERCY

Josef Zawinul

TRACK 25 with drumset   TRACK 26 without drumset

JAZZ LEGENDS AND NOTABLE DRUMMERS

Names to Know

The following is a *partial* list of drummers who were and are vital in the growth and development of jazz. It is the intention of the author to include everyone possible, although omissions are inevitable. For more information on these and many other legendary drummers, check out the Resource section of this book.

Milton Banana
Ray Bauduc
Louie Bellson
Cindy Blackman
Ed Blackwell
Art Blakey
Willie Bobo
Clayton Cameron
Terri Lynn Carrington
"Big" Sid Catlett
Joe Chambers
Mike Clark
Kenny Clarke
Jimmy Cobb
Vinnie Colaiuta
Cozy Cole
Chris Columbus
Mr. Connie Kay
Andrew Cyrille
Alan Dawson
Warren "Baby" Dodds
Frankie Dunlop
Peter Erskine

Steve Gadd
Chico Hamilton
Jeff Hamilton
Lionel Hampton
Jake Hanna
Billy Hart
Roy Haynes
Albert "Tootie" Heath
Billy Higgins
Elvin Jones
Jo Jones
Harold Jones
Philly Joe Jones
Gene Krupa
Joe La Barbera
Don Lamond
Mel Lewis
Edison Machado
Shelly Manne
Butch Miles
Joe Morello
Paul Motian
Sonny Payne

Charli Persip
Buddy Rich
John Riley
Ben Riley
Max Roach
Ed Shaughnessy
Zutty Singleton
Steve Smith
Ed Soph
Bill Stewart
Grady Tate
Arthur Taylor
Ed Thigpen
Dave Tough
Dom Umromao
Jeff Watts
Chick Webb
Dave Weckl
Paul Wertico
George Wettling
Tony Williams
Shadow Wilson
Sam Woodyard

RESOURCES

It is a daunting task to try and list *all* of the important books and recordings of jazz. Undoubtedly, there will be omissions. Therefore, the following is a *partial* listing of resources for gaining a greater understanding of jazz music and its history. Go to your local library or record store and explore many of these and other wonderful resources available on the treasure of jazz!

Jazz Recordings

Notable Albums

Atlantic Jazz: New Orleans (Atlantic)
The Blues: A Smithsonian Collection of Classic Blues Singers (Smithsonian)
The Real Kansas City, 1924–1940 (Sony/Legacy)
An Anthology of Big Band Swing, 1930–1955 (GRP)
Big Band Jazz: From the Beginning to the 1950s (Smithsonian)
Swing Time: The Fabulous Big Band Era, 1925–1955 (Columbia)
Jazz of the 1930s: Greatest Hits (BMG/RCA Victor)
Hot Jazz on a Blue Note (Blue Note/Smithsonian)
Norman Granz' Jazz at the Philharmonic, Vol. 1 and Vol. 2 (Verve)
The Birth of Bebop (Charly-UK)
The Modern Jazz Quartet: Fontessa (Atlantic)
The Original Dixieland Jazz Band, 1917–1921 (Timeless)
King Oliver and His Creole Jazz Band, 1923 (Classics)
The Essential Bessie Smith (Columbia)
Smithsonian Collection of Classic Jazz (Smithsonian)

Notable Artists

Cannonball Adderley
> *Phenix* (Fantasy)
> *Mercy, Mercy, Mercy* (Capitol)

Louis Armstrong
> *Portrait of the Artist as a Young Man (1923–34)* (Legacy/Smithsonian)

Count Basie
> *The Complete Decca Recordings* (Decca)

Bix Beiderbecke
> *His Best Recordings, 1924–1930* (Best of Jazz)

Art Blakey and the Jazz Messengers
> *The History of Art Blakey and the Jazz Messengers* (Blue Note)
> *The Big Beat* (Blue Note)

Dave Brubeck
> *Time Out* (Columbia)
> *Time Signatures: A Career Retrospective 1946–91* (Sony/Legacy)

Benny Carter
> *Further Definitions* (Impulse!)

Betty Carter
> *The Audience with Betty Carter* (Verve)

Ornette Coleman
Beauty Is a Rare Thing: The Complete Atlantic Recordings (Rhino)
The Shape of Jazz to Come (Atlantic)

John Coltrane
A Love Supreme (Impulse! GRP)
Giant Steps (Atlantic)
Live at the Village Vanguard (Impulse!)

Chick Corea
Now He Sings, Now He Sobs (Blue Note)
Music Forever and Beyond (GRP)
Return to Forever: Light as a Feather (Polydor)

Miles Davis
Kind of Blue (Sony/Legacy)
Miles Ahead (Columbia)
The Complete Birth of the Cool (Capitol)
Miles Davis Quintet, 1965–68 (Columbia)
Bitches Brew (Columbia)
Milestones (Columbia)

Duke Ellington
Duke's Men: The Small Groups, Vol. 1 (Columbia)
Far East Suite (Bluebird/RCA)
The Okeh Ellington (Sony/Legacy)
The Blanton-Webster Band (BMG/RCA Victor)

Bill Evans Trio
At the Village Vanguard (Riverside)
Conversations with Myself (Verve)

Ella Fitzgerald
The First Lady of Song (Verve)
Ella in Rome: The Birthday Concert (Verve)

Erroll Garner
Concert by the Sea (Columbia CK)

Stan Getz
Focus (Verve)
The Sound (Roost)
Getz/Gilberto (with Joao Gilberto; Verve)

Dizzy Gillespie
The Complete RCA Victor Recordings (RCA/Bluebird)

Benny Goodman
Live at Carnegie Hall: 1938 Complete (Sony)
The Complete RCA Victor Small Group Recordings (BMG/RCA Victor)

Herbie Hancock
The Best of Herbie Hancock (Blue Note)
Head Hunters (Columbia)
Maiden Voyage (Blue Note)

Coleman Hawkins
A Retrospective, 1929–1963 (Bluebird)
Coleman Hawkins in Europe: 1934–1939 (Timeless)

Woody Herman
The Thundering Herds, 1945–47 (Columbia)

Earl Hines
His Best Recordings, 1927–1942 (Best of Jazz)
The Earl Hines Collection: Piano Solos, 1928–1940 (Collector's Classics)

Billie Holiday
Lady Day: The Complete Billie Holiday on Columbia (1933–1944) (Sony)

Stan Kenton
Retrospective (Capitol)

Joe Lovano
Quartets: Live at the Village Vanguard (Blue Note)

Wynton Marsalis
Marsalis Standard Time, Vol. 1 (Columbia)

Charles Mingus
Passions of a Man: The Complete Atlantic Recordings, 1956–61 (Rhino)
Mingus Ah Um (Legacy)

Thelonious Monk
The Complete Blue Note Recordings (Blue Note)
Thelonious Monk with John Coltrane (Riverside)
Genius of Modern Music, Vol. 2 (Blue Note)
Brilliant Corners (OJC)

Jelly Roll Morton
The Library of Congress Recordings (Rounder)

Gerry Mulligan
The Complete Pacific Jazz Recordings of the Gerry Mulligan Quartet with Chet Baker (Pacific Jazz)

Charlie Parker
Bird and Diz (PolyGram)
Yardbird Suite (Rhino)
Yardbird Suite: The Ultimate Collection (Rhino)

Art Pepper
Art Pepper Meets the Rhythm Section (OJC)

Bud Powell
The Complete Blue Note and Roost Recordings (Blue Note)

Joshua Redman
MoodSwing (Warner Bros.)
Spirit of the Moment—Live at the Village Vanguard (Warner Bros.)

Django Reinhardt
Django Reinhardt, 1935–1936 (Classics)

Max Roach (Clifford Brown and Max Roach)
Alone Together: The Best of the Mercury Years (Verve)
Clifford Brown and Max Roach (EmArcy)
Percussion Bittersweet (Impulse!)

Sonny Rollins
Saxophone Colossus (OJC)
The Bridge (Classic Compact Disc)

Wayne Shorter
>*Speak No Evil* (Blue Note)

Horace Silver
>*Retrospective* (Blue Note)
>*Blowin' the Blues Away* (Blue Note)
>*The Best of Horace Silver, Vol. 1* (Blue Note)

Jimmy Smith
>*The Sermon* (Blue Note)

Sarah Vaughan
>*Swingin' Easy* (EmArcy)

Fats Waller
>*The Joint Is Jumpin'* (RCA Bluebird)

Weather Report
>*Heavy Weather* (Columbia)

Lester Young
>*Kansas City Sessions* (GRP)

Latin Recordings

This is a partial listing! Many of these and other recordings are available online.

Antonio Carlos Jobim
>*Verve Jazz Masters 13* (PolyGram)
>*Girl from Ipanema: The Antonio Carlos Jobim Songbook* (PolyGram)
>*Wave* (A&M)

Stan Getz
>*Stan Getz and Joao Gilberto* (PolyGram)
>*Jazz Samba: Charlie Byrd and Stan Getz* (Verve)

Samba Schools / Carnival
>*Batucada Brasiliera: The Great Rhythms of Brazillian Samba Schools* (Cid)
>*Batucada Brasiliera: School of Samba Mocidade* (IRIS Music)
>*Batucada Sound of the Favelas* (Mr. Bongo)
>*Batucada Fatastica: Luciano Perrone/Nilo Sergio* (Musicdisc)

Airto Morera
>*Essential: The Very Best of Airto Morera* (Nascente Records)

Bebel Gilberto
>*Tanto Tempo* (Six Degrees)

Celia Cruz
>*Celia Cruz and Friends: A Night of Salsa* (RMM Records)
>*100% Azcura: The Best of Celia Cruz and La Sonora Matancera* (Rhino Records)

Tito Puente and His Orchestra
>*The Complete RCA Recordings, Vols. 1 and 2* (RCA International)
>*Dance Mania Volume 1* (RCA International)

Various
>*This Is Jazz, Volume 29: Bossa Nova* (Sony)
>*La Senora Mantancera: 65 Anniversario* (Ofreon Records)

Texts

Timekeepers: The Great Jazz Drummers; Leslie Gourse
Drummin' Men: The Heartbeat of Jazz, The Swing Era; Burt Korrall
Drummin' Men: The Heartbeat of Jazz, The Bebop Years; Burt Korrall
Jazz: The First Century; John Edward Hasse
The NPR Curious Listener's Guide to Jazz; Loren Schoenberg
Jazz: The American Theme Song; James Lincoln Collier
Jazz Styles; Mark Gridley
The Swing Era: The Development of Jazz 1930–1945; Gunther Schuller
Blues People; Leroi Jones
Ragtime: A Musical and Cultural History; Edward Berlin
Zildjian: A History of the Legendary Cymbal Makers; Jon Cohan

DVD / Video

Classic Jazz Drummers: Swing and Beyond; Hudson Music
Drum Solos & Battles: Part 1 and Part 2; Hudson Music
Legends of Jazz Drumming: Part 1, 1920–1950; DCI Video
Legends of Jazz Drumming: Part 2, 1950–1970; DCI Video
Gene Krupa: Swing, Swing, Swing; Hudson Music
Jazz Legend: Gene Krupa; DCI Video
Buddy Rich: At the Top; Hudson Music
Buddy Rich: Jazz Legend Part 1, 1917–1970; Warner Bros.
Buddy Rich: Jazz Legend Part 2, 1970–1987; Warner Bros.
Buddy Rich and His Band: The Lost West Side Story Tapes; Hudson Music
Elvin Jones: Different Drummer; CPP Media
Elvin Jones: Jazz Machine; View Video
Steve Smith: Drumset Technique/History of the U.S. Beat; Hudson Music
Peter Erskine: Timekeeping and Everything Is Timekeeping; DCI Video
The Peter Erskine Trio: Live at Jazz Baltica; Hudson Music
Clayton Cameron: Live at PAS; CPP Media
Ed Thigpen: The Essence of Brushes; CPP Media
Jack DeJohnette: Musical Expression on the Drumset; Homespun Video
Louie Bellson: Louie Bellson Big Band; View Video
Louie Bellson: The Musical Drummer; DCI Video
Johnny Vidacovich Street Beats: Modern Applications; DCI Video
New Orleans Drumming: Boxed Set; DCI Video

Instructional Books: Drumset

There are many drumset instructional books available on the subject of jazz. The following is a partial list of excellent resources designed to teach and strengthen jazz drumming techniques and coordination.

Creative Timekeeping, Rick Mattingly
Advanced Techniques for the Modern Drummer, Jim Chapin
The Drummer's Complete Vocabulary, as taught by Alan Dawson, John Ramsay
The Art of Bop Drumming, John Riley
Beyond Bop Drumming, John Riley
Essential Techniques for Drumset, Ed Soph
Jazz Drumming, Billy Hart
The Great Jazz Drummers, Ron Spagnardi

The Complete Rhythm Section, Steve Houghton
The Sound of Brushes, Ed Thigpen
Drumset Essentials: Vols. 1–3, Peter Erskine

Jazz Standard Tune Books

The chart books listed below contain a *wealth* of jazz standard and modern jazz tunes. Although all are used frequently in the performance of jazz, *The Real Book: Volume 1* is likely to be the most commonly used.

The Real Book: Volume 1 (Hal Leonard, HL00240221)
The Real Book: Volume 2 (Hal Leonard, HL00240222)
The Real Book: Volume 3 (Hal Leonard, HL00240233)
The New Real Book: Volume 1 (Sher Music/Hal Leonard, HL00242103)
The New Real Book: Volume 2 (Sher Music/Hal Leonard, HL00242106)
The New Real Book: Volume 3 (Sher Music/Hal Leonard, HL00242109)

BIBLIOGRAPHY

Hasse, John Edward. *Jazz: The First Century.*
    Harper Collins Publishers, 2000

Schoenberg, Loren. *The NPR Curious Listener's Guide to Jazz.*
    Grand Central Press and National Public Radio, 2002

Riley, John. *The Art of Bop Drumming.*
    Manhattan Music Publications, 1994

Mattingly, Rick. *Creative Timekeeping for the Contemporary Jazz Drummer.*
    Hal Leonard, 1992

Black, Dave / Fullen, Brian. *Bass Drum Essentials for the Drumset.*
    Alfred Publishing Co., 2001

Cohan, Jon. *A History of the Legendary Cymbal Makers.*
    Hal Leonard, 1999

Gridley, Mark C. *Jazz Styles.*
    Prentice-Hall, Inc., 1978

Berry, Mick / Gianni, Jason. *The Drummer's Bible.*
    See Sharp Press, 2004

YOU CAN'T BEAT OUR DRUM BOOKS!

Bass Drum Control
Best Seller for More Than 50 Years!
by Colin Bailey
This perennial favorite among drummers helps players develop their bass drum technique and increase their flexibility through the mastery of exercises.
06620020 Book/Online Audio $17.99

The Complete Drumset Rudiments
by Peter Magadini
Use your imagination to incorporate these rudimental etudes into new patterns that you can apply to the drumset or tom toms as you develop your hand technique with the Snare Drum Rudiments, your hand and foot technique with the Drumset Rudiments and your polyrhythmic technique with the Polyrhythm Rudiments. Adopt them all into your own creative expressions based on ideas you come up with while practicing.
06620016 Book/CD Pack $14.95

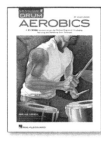

Drum Aerobics
by Andy Ziker
A 52-week, one-exercise-per-day workout program for developing, improving, and maintaining drum technique. Players of all levels – beginners to advanced – will increase their speed, coordination, dexterity and accuracy. The online audio contains all 365 workout licks, plus play-along grooves in styles including rock, blues, jazz, heavy metal, reggae, funk, calypso, bossa nova, march, mambo, New Orleans 2nd Line, and lots more!
06620137 Book/Online Audio $19.99

Drumming the Easy Way!
The Beginner's Guide to Playing Drums for Students and Teachers
by Tom Hapke
Cherry Lane Music
Now with online audio! This book takes the beginning drummer through the paces – from reading simple exercises to playing great grooves and fills. Each lesson includes a preparatory exercise and a solo. Concepts and rhythms are introduced one at a time, so growth is natural and easy. Features large, clear musical print, intensive treatment of each individual drum figure, solos following each exercise to motivate students, and more!
02500876 Book/Online Audio...$19.99
02500191 Book..$14.99

The Drumset Musician – 2nd Edition
by Rod Morgenstein and Rick Mattingly
Containing hundreds of practical, usable beats and fills, *The Drumset Musician* teaches you how to apply a variety of patterns and grooves to the actual performance of songs. The accompanying online audio includes demos as well as 18 play-along tracks covering a wide range of rock, blues and pop styles, with detailed instructions on how to create exciting, solid drum parts.
00268369 Book/Online Audio..$19.99

www.halleonard.com

Instant Guide to Drum Grooves
The Essential Reference for the Working Drummer
by Maria Martinez
Become a more versatile drumset player! From traditional Dixieland to cutting-edge hip-hop, *Instant Guide to Drum Grooves* is a handy source featuring 100 patterns that will prepare working drummers for the stylistic variety of modern gigs. The book includes essential beats and grooves in such styles as: jazz, shuffle, country, rock, funk, New Orleans, reggae, calypso, Brazilian and Latin.
06620056 Book/CD Pack $12.99

1001 Drum Grooves
The Complete Resource for Every Drummer
by Steve Mansfield
Cherry Lane Music
This book presents 1,001 drumset beats played in a variety of musical styles, past and present. It's ideal for beginners seeking a well-organized, easy-to-follow encyclopedia of drum grooves, as well as consummate professionals who want to bring their knowledge of various drum styles to new heights. Author Steve Mansfield presents: rock and funk grooves, blues and jazz grooves, ethnic grooves, Afro-Cuban and Caribbean grooves, and much more.
02500337 Book...$14.99

Polyrhythms – The Musician's Guide
by Peter Magadini
edited by Wanda Sykes
Peter Magadini's *Polyrhythms* is acclaimed the world over and has been hailed by *Modern Drummer* magazine as "by far the best book on the subject." Written for instrumentalists and vocalists alike, this book with online audio contains excellent solos and exercises that feature polyrhythmic concepts. Topics covered include: 6 over 4, 5 over 4, 7 over 4, 3 over 4, 11 over 4, and other rhythmic ratios; combining various polyrhythms; polyrhythmic time signatures; and much more. The audio includes demos of the exercises and is accessed online using the unique code in each book.
06620053 Book/Online Audio..$19.99

Joe Porcaro's Drumset Method – Groovin' with Rudiments
Patterns Applied to Rock, Jazz & Latin Drumset
by Joe Porcaro
Master teacher Joe Porcaro presents rudiments at the drumset in this sensational new edition of *Groovin' with Rudiments*. This book is chock full of exciting drum grooves, sticking patterns, fills, polyrhythmic adaptations, odd meters, and fantastic solo ideas in jazz, rock, and Latin feels. The online audio features 99 audio clip examples in many styles to round out this true collection of superb drumming material for every serious drumset performer.
06620129 Book/Online Audio $24.99

66 Drum Solos for the Modern Drummer
Rock • Funk • Blues • Fusion • Jazz
by Tom Hapke
Cherry Lane Music
66 Drum Solos for the Modern Drummer presents drum solos in all styles of music in an easy-to-read format. These solos are designed to help improve your technique, independence, improvisational skills, and reading ability on the drums and at the same time provide you with some cool licks that you can use right away in your own playing.
02500319 Book/Online Audio..$17.99

HAL•LEONARD®

Prices, contents, and availability subject to change without notice.

00672527	**Audioslave**		$24.95
00672378	**The Beatles – Transcribed Scores**		$24.95
00673208	**Best of Blood, Sweat & Tears**		$24.99
00672367	**Chicago – Volume 1**		$24.99
00672368	**Chicago – Volume 2**		$29.99
00672452	**Miles Davis – Birth of the Cool**		$29.99
00672460	**Miles Davis – Kind of Blue (Sketch Scores)**		$19.99
00672502	**Deep Purple – Greatest Hits**		$27.99
00672427	**Ben Folds Five – Selections from Naked Baby Photos**		$24.99
00672428	**Ben Folds Five – Whatever and Ever, Amen**		$27.99
00001333	**Getz/Gilberto**		$29.99
00672308	**Jimi Hendrix – Are You Experienced?**		$32.99
00672345	**Jimi Hendrix – Axis Bold As Love**		$29.95
00672397	**Jimi Hendrix – Experience Hendrix**		$35.00
00672465	**John Lennon – Imagine**		$24.95
00672541	**Pat Metheny Group – The Way Up**		$29.99
00690582	**Nickel Creek – Nickel Creek**		$24.99

00672501	**The Police – Greatest Hits**		$24.95
00672538	**The Best of Queen**		$27.50
00672515	**Red Hot Chili Peppers – By the Way**		$24.95
00672456	**Red Hot Chili Peppers – Californication**		$24.95
00672536	**Red Hot Chili Peppers – Greatest Hits**		$24.95
00001591	**Red Hot Chili Peppers – I'm With You**		$27.99
00672551	**Red Hot Chili Peppers – Stadium Arcadium**		$49.95
00672360	**Santana's Greatest Hits**		$29.99
02500283	**Joe Satriani – Greatest Hits**		$24.95
00675170	**The Best of Spyro Gyra**		$24.99
00675200	**The Best of Steely Dan**		$24.99
00675520	**Best of Weather Report**		$24.99

HAL•LEONARD®
www.halleonard.com
Prices, contents, and availability
subject to change without notice.

0222
178